MW00412637

REDEFINE YOUR WEDDING BUSINESS

Create the Business You Want Wherever You Are

ANDREA EPPOLITO

© ANDREA EPPOLITO. ALL RIGHTS RESERVED

All rights reserved. No part of this book may be reproduced in any form without written permission in advance from the publisher and author. International rights and translations are available solely at the discretion of and through agreement with Andrea Eppolito Events LLC and The Editorial Collective.

To inquire about permission for use of material content in this book, please contact:

Andrea Eppolito
11035 Lavender Hill Drive
Suite 160-245
Las Vegas, Nevada 89135
(702) 604-1857
admin@andreaeppolito.com

Printed in the Unites States of America
ISBN 978-1-54398-798-0

To learn more about Andrea Eppolito and the education available, please visit www.andreaeppolito.com.

DEDICATION

To Tony
My partner in business and in life.
Without you, none of it means anything.

To Anthony & Alexandria
Everything I do is for you. I hope I make you proud, and
that I leave you a city (and a world) that is better that it was
when I found it.

To the Wedding Community
I love this industry. I love the work I do,
who I do it for, and who I do it with.
Thank you for everything.

TABLE OF CONTENTS

TABLE OF CONTENTS

INTRODUCTION

Throughout my life, I've started and stopped writing a number of books. There was the love story I began writing as a teenager, the book of poetry that I finished in my early 20s, at least two other books on the wedding industry, and one autobiographical piece that I've never been able to properly put into words.

And yet this is the first book that I have ever been able to sit and write from beginning to end with absolutely no interruptions. If there's anything I'm known for in the wedding industry, it is that I redefined what it means to get married in Las Vegas. I entered the industry at a time when Las Vegas was known more for the $.99 shrimp cocktail and drive-through Elvis Wedding Chapels than it was for luxury, opulence, and production. And yet those were the things that I loved. That was the work that I wanted to do, and I was determined to do it here, in this city that I loved.

In 2010, I wrote out a business plan and a list of goals.

The first goal was to be the best wedding planner in Las Vegas. The second goal was to redefine what it meant to get married in Las Vegas.

As ego driven (and subjective) as the first goal was, it was the driving force behind all of my work. I knew that I would never be allowed to do the work I wanted to do if I tried to operate as a unicorn, out there on my own, sitting on a long tree branch all by myself.

The entire market would need to change for all of the creatives in our community and the profile of the entire city needed to be elevated in order to support the platform that I wanted to work from.

When I started my business, the most expensive wedding planners in Las Vegas were charging on average $3,500 - $5,000 for full planning services. Today, my average fee is more than ten times that amount, and most wedding planners in Las Vegas now have full planning packages starting at $10,000. Ten years ago, seeing a Las Vegas wedding featured on a blog or in print was practically unheard of. Today, myself and my colleagues routinely have the honor of seeing our work featured in the national press. In the beginning, the idea of a luxury wedding in Las Vegas was at best a rarity and at worst a punchline. Today, upscale wedding planners in my city are no longer struggling to find clients with six-figure budgets. Instead, we are able to confidently command real dollars and we justify those budgets easily based on the quality of our work and the press that it generates. We have successfully raised the bar, setting both the standard and the minimum of our market at a significantly higher price point for both local weddings and destination weddings alike.

I can wholeheartedly say that I am running the business of my dreams. As a wedding planner and event designer, I work with an intimate client base that cares deeply about production and atmosphere. My clients trust me to bend the universe to their will, and they invest the financial means that allow me to do just that. Together, we do things that have never been done before. I wake up every day excited by the work that I get to do and the possibilities of what could come next. I make the money that I want to make, the money that I deserve. My work is published internationally, and the opportunities that have been created because of that have taken me all over the world. Every day is a dream come true professionally.

The larger joy, and what I am most proud of, is that the entire city of Las Vegas now has a higher profile in our industry. Las Vegas has enjoyed a newfound respect as a high-end wedding destination that is both worthy and capable of producing luxury events for discerning couples from around the world.

It's taken me almost a full decade to get to a place where I am consistently able to do the work that I want to do. While traveling the world as a speaker and educator, I am often stopped after my presentation by an attendee who laments, "Yeah, it's great in Las Vegas, but I live in (insert city)," to which my reply is always, "So what?"

Las Vegas is a city built upon sand and dreams born from a

thought, a massive amount of innovation, and tireless work. Everything in this city has been conjured and created. If an entire city could be built on an idea, I thought, surely I could build the type of business that I wanted. Furthermore, if I wanted to do this type of work in this place, then surely other people would want to experience it as well. I knew I couldn't possibly be alone in the desire to do something other than what I was seeing. Thankfully, I was right.

And so much like the city that I have come to call home, I took an idea and I brought it to life through determination, sheer will, and a relentless pursuit of the things I wanted most.

If I was able to redefine my business, and my local market, then you certainly can redefine yours! Whether you live in a major city or a small town, an hour outside of New York City or three hours away from the nearest airport in California, you have the power and the talent to transform both your business and your community. This book will take you step-by-step through the process of how I did just that.

As an industry, we are both the seekers and the doers. We are the makers of dreams come true. We stand on the sidelines and witness the most intimate of all life's moments. Our businesses exist to celebrate others. We traffic in intimacy, and our relationships are forged in fire. The emotional investment we make in our clients and our work is extraordinary, and for that type of emotional investment, we deserve to run businesses we love.

I don't care who you are, what baggage you bring to the table, or where you are located. If there is work that you want to see and things you want to do, then I absolutely guarantee that there are other people who want what you want. There are wedding professionals who want to do the same work that you want to do.

We have a responsibility to ourselves, our clients, and our industry as a whole to consistently move the needle. Wherever that needle is, it's yours. Move it to the place you feel most alive.

DEFINING SUCCESS

Are you set up for success? Not only in your business, but in life?

Well, that's a loaded question. Success is defined differently for each of us. For some wedding pros, success means continued growth. They want to take on more clients each year, growing their teams, adding employees, and adding offices throughout the country. For others, success is defined in dollars. Many businesses have an annual revenue number to hit and they determine whether or not they have done a good job by how far under or over they are in relation to that number. Still, other businesses determine success by the amount of press that they receive, their ability to be featured, and whether or not they have access to a celebrity level of clientele.

I can't tell you what success will mean in your business, but I want to share with you what it means for me. My husband and I have always started with what we wanted our life to look like, and then we retrofit the business in order to support that. For us, we want to have the ability to spend time with our children. It has always been important to us that we take them to school, pick them up, and that we have dinner together most nights of the week. We wanted to be involved parents who could attend school functions and activities. It was also very important to us that we set aside time for ourselves as a couple. Financially, of course we set goals for ourselves. For example, we have a certain amount of money that we need to make each month in order to support our lifestyle. But we also want to set aside money for travel, retirement, and what my husband likes to call "creature comforts" that we can enjoy together.

Personally, I have always been a fan of what I like to call "f*ck you" money. This is the money that buys you freedom. The freedom to walk away from any job that you don't want to take, the freedom to pass on a client that is not serving your business. This is what buys you peace of mind, knowing that if you have a slow season one year, which we all have in the course of our business, that you are going to be OK.

Professionally, I define success by being able to do the kind of work that I want to do, with clients that see the world the same way that I do. I don't care about volume; in fact, I avoid it. My ideal client is one who cares about environment and atmosphere. I am a dreamer, and I seek to create the world that I wish I lived in. My clients are also dreamers, and together we bend the universe to our will, designing and creating once in a lifetime spaces that tell stories, that entice the five senses, and that speak to who they are as a couple. I want to change people at their core, to inspire them to live beautifully, and I want these moments we share together to become memories that last a lifetime. When I open up the doors to a wedding with 100 invited guests, they belong to me. For that one night the world is a perfectly beautiful place. Watching their faces as they enter a room, listening to them "ooh" and "ahh" over a centerpiece or statement ceiling, and seeing them chant for one more song defines my success. Reading Thank You notes from the Father of the Bride who has worked his whole life to give his daughter this moment, and getting random text messages three years later that say, "As beautiful as your last wedding was, mine is still my favorite" defines my success as a wedding planner.

Do these goals need to be your goals? Of course not. Success in your business and in your life is going to depend solely on you.

How will you define success? Think about what you want your life to feel like on a day-to-day basis. Take out a piece of paper, and write out the answers to the following questions:

> What are the main priorities in your life?
> When and where do you feel your best?
> What responsibilities do you have to your family and to your friends on a day-to-day basis?
> How much time do you want to spend managing your clients?
> How much time would you like to spend in your business?

What are your financial goals?
What would you like to accomplish in your life
outside of your business?

Burn out happens when your business takes over your life,
and when your business fails to help you be the person
that you want to be. These answers are going to be deeply
personal, and you should write them out without any
judgment. Your priorities could be building a business
while having time to travel for at least six weeks out of each
year. You may feel your best while sitting at a computer
editing images, or rushing from one event to another
because nothing beats that adrenaline high. You may be
the sole provider for a family of three, who needs you to
be available for school pick up and drop-offs. You could
be single, but care deeply about spending time with your
friends. You could be married, with no children and able to
dedicate all of your time Monday through Friday 8:00 A.M.
to 7:00 P.M. to do your all of your work. Your financial
goals may be modest, or over the top, and perhaps the only
thing you really want to do in your life is help others create
memories for themselves.

The point is that there is no right answer but your answer
is going to determine how you set up your business. Once
you've spent time thinking about the life that you want to
lead, I want you to apply those goals and priorities to your
business and take inventory of your successes and failures.
Has your business grown so large that it takes up all of your
time, leaving little if any downtime that allows you to read?
Are you working with clients who don't pay you enough to
reach your financial goals? Is your schedule so packed that

you haven't taken a vacation in the last two years?

Once you've taken a look at the current state of your business, it's time to re-design your work life to support your real life. I want you to fill in the blanks to the following:

I am a(n): _____

_____

My job is to: _____

_____

My business will work with _____
(number) of clients who will pay me between
$_____ and $_____
each

My Total Annual Revenue will be
$_____

I care deeply about _____

_____

My clients know that I can create _____, _____,
and _____ for them.

If you're stuck on how to answer these questions and fill in the blanks, take a look at some of the samples that I've worked through with other professionals.

"I am a florist. My job is to provide my clients with simple and sweet centerpieces and floral accents that complement their style. My business will work with 100 clients each year, who will pay me between $7,000 and $10,000 each. My Total Annual Revenue will be $700,000 to $1,000,000. I care deeply about making sure that every couple has a beautiful wedding, and my clients know that I can create an elegant wedding, beautiful bouquets, and personal touches at any price point for them."

"I am a wedding entertainer. My job is to provide my clients with over-the-top production and amazing music that keeps their guests raging on the dance floor all night long. My business will work with forty to fifty couples each year, and they will pay me between $5,000 and $12,000 per event with a total revenue goal of $450,000. I care deeply about making sure that music changes the energy of the room, and that we provide a playlist that is appropriate for all the stages of the event. My clients know that I will play a mix of romantic ballads, classical tunes, and that I have the ability to read a room and adjust the music to their guests' needs."

Understanding how you define success in your life will determine how you set up your business. Once you've determined what you want, the next step is identifying what clients will bring this to your business.

VISUALIZE YOUR IDEAL MARKET

Redefining your market requires you to know where you are, and where you want do go.

This journey begins with the destination in mind. You have to know where it is that you want to go before you can chart the course on how you will get there.

Step one is visualization. Visualization is a powerful tool; not to be confused with any New Age, juju-style secret or wishing upon a star. This is about designing the business and the life that you want.

To do this, you will need to consider both the micro and the macro. The micro is about your business, specifically; while the macro is your market and the industry at large.

Start first with the micro and design your ideal client and business. Ask yourself the following:

What type of work do I want to do?
Who is my ideal client?
What needs does this client have?
What problem does my client need me to solve?
What unique products and services can I offer?
How will my work exceed my client's
expectations?
How will my client base differ from that of
competition?
How will my work be distinguishable from the
work of my strongest competitor?
What price point do I want to work with, and why?
How much of the overall budget do I want my
services to account for?
What value does this investment bring to my
clients?

Notice how the bulk of these questions are surrounding your
clients.

Our clients are the life blood of our businesses. Without
them, we do not exist in this world. Therefore, when seeking
to redefine an industry and build the business that you want
to run, you must start with the end user. If you make every
decision based on the deepest needs and desires of your
couples, then you can't go wrong.

Consider building out an avatar of sorts. Imagine your ideal
client. Write about them. Who they are? What they do?
Where did they go to school, and how do they operate in the
world? What is their world view? What do they care about?

Now, go deeper. Imagine your ideal client on a regular day. Imagine them waking up; what time is it? Is it light outside, or still dark? Do they start their day with a work out, or do they rush right to the office? When they get dressed, what brands specifically do they wear? Imagine them grocery shopping. Is it all organic, or do they favor pre-made meals that can be easily thrown together? What do they consider entertainment? There is a vast difference between sports enthusiasts and the "Netflix and chill" types, and even a greater divide between your homebody book reader and your festival goer.

Your ideal client profile could read as follows:

> Both members of my ideal couple are professionals, with a college education and a deep-seated desire to succeed. They make in the high six figures each year, and they are insatiable in their desire to succeed, grow, and advance. My couples love to travel, enjoy dining out, and they love live music and entertainment. While they are educated, they really care about the emotional aspect of their lives, and they want to make people feel a certain way. The ideal client for my business is family-oriented, and they have close relationships with all of the people in their lives. They wear a mix of high fashion accessories and shop at high-end retailers. They own their home, or will be buying one in the future. They care about the opinions of others, and want to make a statement.

Or, perhaps your client profile read something more like this:

My ideal clients are deeply committed to one another, and want to share their love with their closest family and friends. Neither is comfortable being the center of attention, and instead want to put the emphasis on the guest experience. They are homebodies, most comfortable cooking dinner, binge-watching their favorite shows, and entertaining small groups of people. They work to live, but don't live to work. My clients shop at Target and the farmers market, and they care about sustainability. Giving back is important to them, and they would be incredibly uncomfortable with anything overly demonstrative or produced.

The planner in me loves a good mood board. Whether you go old school and create a tangible board with photos and cut outs or if you build a digital representation, you should have a profile built around your ideal couple. This is who your business is for. These are the people you will speak to, and your work is only for them. Every decision you make from this point forward is going to be in the best interest of your client avatar.

Once your client avatar is built, turn your attention to the business model itself. As much as our businesses exist to serve our clients, they also exist to support the lifestyle that we as individuals wish to lead. How you build and run your business is important in terms of your quality of life and your ability to exist without burn out. Each one of us has a unique set of responsibilities, motivators, and goals. What I want for my own life as a mother, wife, and business owner is wildly different from what every other business owner and operator I meet needs.

This is an incredibly intimate exercise, but it is one of the most valuable things you can do to shape your future. Walk yourself through a series of questions. Feel free to ignore what does not apply to you, and add in anything of value that you feel is missing.

> For me, being a successful _____ means _____.
>
> I want to work _____ days a week.
> My day will being at _____ and end at _____.
> For me to be happy, I must have time for _____.
>
> Being a good spouse / partner / friend means:
> Being a good parent means:
> I need to make _____ in order to support my current lifestyle.
> I want to make _____ so that I can live the life I want, which includes _____, _____, and _____.

As an example, one of my first attempts at walking through this exercise read:

> For me, being a successful wedding planner means that I can work with a small number of couples that care about creating a unique environment. I want to make a living and have a life. I don't mind working 7 days a week; in fact, I love it! But I want to have ownership and control over when I work.
>
> For me to be happy, I must find a way to be a

business owner, and a wife and mother. If I fail at my marriage or as a mom, none of my professional successes will matter. But if I walk away from the work that I am passionate about I know I will be unhappy, frustrated, and resentful.

I want to be available to my kids in the mornings and afternoons. I want to be the mom who helps with homework and shows up at games, and I also want to cook family dinners and sit at the table together. I want to give my husband some one-on-one time each week and maybe take a date night every two months.

I would love to find time to read, to work out, and just to think in a quiet place.

After looking at what I wanted for my life, I was able to retrofit my business to support it. My day starts early (typically before the kids are up), but the bulk of my work happens while they are in school. I don't mind starting and stopping my work flow in order to accommodate their schedules, and I don't mind working after hours or late night to finish my to-do list.

Will this structure work for you? Only you can answer that. What matters most is that you develop one that does work for you.

Now that you have developed both your ideal business and your ideal client in the micro, broaden your gaze and take in the market as a whole. What would your market look like in a perfect world? Envision the type of community you want to work in. Take the time to walk yourself through the following series of questions and write out your answers:

What do I wish this market was known for?
What types of couples do I wish were drawn to this market?
What priorities would the ideal couple have?
When people talk about weddings in this location, what adjectives do I want them to use?
How would the media describe the average wedding in my city?
How often would I like to see my market featured in the press, and where?

Complete the visualization process by placing your ideal client in your ideal market. For this to work, all elements must be in alignment; your ideal business should support the needs of your ideal client, and your market should be a place where both can thrive. If you have done the work from a thoughtful and authentic place, then you should easily imagine the client of your dreams being drawn to the market you seek to create. If, however, you encounter any area where there is resistance or a gap, go back through the questions and ask yourself what needs to change in order to pull every element together in a way that makes sense.

STATE OF THE UNION

With the image of your perfect world business, client, and market firmly held in your mind, it's time to shift focus to the reality of your environment. This is not about judgment, but identifying the gaps that exist in all three.

Begin with your clients. Identify the last three to five clients that you enjoyed working with the most. Create a profile of your current client based on the criteria that was set for your avatar. Create a profile on each client that answers the questions we posed to your avatar.

My favorite clients in the last year were
_____.

I loved the work we did together because
_____.

What problems did I solve for this couple, and how?

This couple chose me because _____.

I exceeded my client's expectations by _____.

I feel that I fell short in my overall goals because _____.

I was paid _____ for my work.

Looking back, the true value of my work on this wedding was _____.

Next, review the current state of your business in relation to both your ideal model and your market. Think about the financial state of your business, the processes, and the administration.

Then, review the work you created on behalf of your client. Be as specific as possible. Force yourself to be brutally honest in assessing your strengths and weaknesses. Ask yourself the following:

How is my business described by my peers?
How do my couples find me?
What needs do these couples have?
Why do couples choose me over my competition?
What do I do that is different from the rest of my market?
Is my branding unique?
Does it stand out in my market?
How many couples do I serve each year?

Do I want to work with more or less?

How much money do I make per couple?

What value does this investment bring to my
clients?

As you work through these questions, your goal is to
identify the void. Where do you fall short of your goal? In
what ways is your business not set up for success? What is
it about your market that is a benefit to your ideal client, and
what does it lack? Journaling through the process will help
you understand the gap between where you are, and where
you want to be.

Pay attention to the way you feel while you write. Our
work is driven by emotions, and the personal investment
you make in the industry cannot and should not be ignored.
Books and your brain will only take you so far. Changes
happen when you feel something. Be vulnerable and honest
with yourself.

When I look back through my old notes, I have entries that
read:

I'm doing a lot of good work, but I wish I were
doing more great work.

On one hand, I'm struggling to understand why
other planners are getting more business than I,
but when I look at the work that they are doing,
I'm not sure that it's what I want to do. Are luxury
weddings just not valued here? Does anyone want
what I do? Where are they?

I keep paying for all this advertising, but I'm not converting leads.

Why isn't my work being published? I really believe that my weddings are as good as the other weddings I see on popular blogs. What am I missing?

I want to stop taking "regular" weddings, but I'm afraid I won't be able to support myself without the income.

Each of these statements was absolutely true at the time that I wrote them. As I look back at them now, I can see that they are rooted in fear, insecurity, and lack of confidence. Look at them again, and see if you notice the pattern.

"I wish I were doing more..."
"Does anyone want what I do?"
"Why isn't my work being published?
"What am I missing?"

As sad as I am to have ever been in that place, I know two things: The first is that without having been there, I would never have gotten here. The second is that I will be there, back in that place, again.

The challenge and the beauty of owning your own business, while also being an artist is that there will always be a gap. We never fully arrive. As an industry, we are 24 hour heroes, judged solely on our last event, forever chasing the next place.

This limbo is the gap. Many of us view the gap as a negative, and we see it as an obstacle that stops us from reaching our goals. Nothing could be further from the truth! The gap is actually the place where you will excel. It's where all of the opportunities are. Once you identify the gaps in your own business, and in your market, you will see that there are clients not being served. Businesses are successful based on their ability to fill a void. Once you realize this, you can begin to address the gaps that exist in your market place and create products and services that can fill them.

In the last chapter, you were asked to imagine your ideal market. Now, having looked into your client base and your own business model, it's time to address how what you are doing contributes to the state of your overall market. Recognize that the work you do is impacting your community, and begin to frame the gap as an opportunity and a need that can showcase your services.

For example, perhaps you are in a place where your business or your market is associated with smaller weddings that are semi-formal, when what you really want is to be doing larger weddings that are formal or black tie. Identify the gap in a way that allows you to fill it by saying:

"By focusing on smaller weddings with semi-formal styling, we are failing to provide services to all of those couples who want a more luxurious experience. This year, I will encourage one couple to add another layer of design or experience to their wedding weekend. This will give my partners the opportunity to do exciting, new things while showing that the market can create this type of experience."

Our business models and our lives are similar in that they are in a constant state of transformation. You have the power and the ability to change the business you have and the market you work in. You cannot, however, do it alone.

CREATING A COMMUNITY

In order to move the needle, you will need to create a community of like-minded partnerships.

One of the issues that smaller businesses have in transforming their market is that there is a lack of local support for the grand vision. This voice is felt by clients who then perceive it to be a lack of talent. By not creating and celebrating a sense of local community, we as an industry tell our couples that we do not have the local skill to support their vision. We instill fear by allowing for the unknown, and our potential clients respond by going elsewhere.

Fight against this by building a community of peers and partners that share your vision for the future. You must actively seek out like-minded individuals and invite people to share your vision for the future.

Communities are built around shared beliefs and the idea

that the future can be better than it is today. For your community to take root and then be successful, you must bring people together by creating a promise and a plan.

Start by identifying local businesses and peers whose work you admire. You want to create a culture of influence, where each of you champions the other's work in order to leverage your standing in the community. The first part of this is about social proof and linking your business to the businesses of those that you admire in your market. The second part of the equation is creating a network of like-minded individuals that are already scratching the surface of the type of work you want to do. By coming together, you will have greater creative energies. The collective force of your efforts will be magnified, helping each of you (and your community at-large) move further together than you could alone.

If you already have relationships with them, strengthen them by reaching out every two weeks with a call or email to touch base. When you see a company whose work you admire, open the door to communication by starting to follow them on social media. Like, comment, and direct message your praise and ask them thoughtful questions about how their business runs and where they would like two be in the future. Get to know the needs and desires of your potential partners so that you can be a part of their future growth and success.

The goal at this stage is to make yourself as useful to the community as possible. If you see a tutorial on bridal make up that you find interesting, send it to your local beauty team and ask them their thoughts. If an image keeps crossing your feed, ask a local photographer what they think about it and whether or not they would be interested in doing work like this. Share information, ask questions, and allow others to show their expertise. Make your partners feel special by researching their business. Look for commonalities such as shared connections and interests. Everyone wants to feel valued and important, and by showing that you care about the work of others you will create a sense of trust.

Once you begin to develop one-on-one relationships, start making connections. Introduce a venue manager to a videographer, and perhaps take them both for coffee. Suggest that a planner visit a new coffee spot to hear someone play, and go with them. Invite all of the vendors from your last wedding to a "thank you" breakfast. Keep things light and fun at first. Allow everyone to get to know one another. Never force a connection or try to create a sense of community where there is none. If two people are unable to talk easily or if their interactions feel strained, that will slow the process of change and create conflict. Instead, focus on developing and finding common ground in the business that you are doing today, and begin talking about the business you would like to do in the future.

As your relationships fall into place, it is up to you to create a culture. Do this deliberately by openly talking about the work that you want to do. Focus on the type of work that you can all do together. Ask your partners about the changes they want to make in their businesses, and create buy-in by focusing on the shared benefit you will receive by partnering together. Strengthen your bonds by creating a trade of in-kind agreement that you can rely on to sell one another's services. For example, a florist may offer complimentary boutonnières to any wedding party that a planner sends. Or, a photo team may offer a venue large prints for every three weddings that the manager refers.

Agreements like this benefit the clients as they are able to stretch the value of their investment and get more for their money.

More importantly, they strengthen the community by establishing that this new network of creatives partner together on a regular basis and do amazing work as a result. And lastly, by each individual business giving something small, it elevates the entire look and feel of the wedding. Everyone's work collectively looks better as a result, attracting the right clients to each of your businesses, where you will then refer them within your community.

STORYTELLING TO YOUR IDEAL CLIENT

How do we engage our ideal client and inspire them to invest in a completely irrational purchase? We tell them a story.

Storytelling is the tie that binds us, connecting one generation to the next. Stories connect us to our humanity.

Our clients seek to engage with us based on their humanity, their world view, and the desire they have to celebrate. This is true, regardless of whether you plan to work with a standard client hosting an average-priced wedding or a luxury client that is going to spend in the high six- and seven-figures on their wedding. At the most basic level your guests are going to have the same need to celebrate, to document their lives, and to create a legacy of who they are in their community.

Remember! People don't buy things or services. People

buy feelings.

When you begin to market your services, you want to focus on what your clients want, rather than what you think they need. Buying in the wedding space is not logical; it's emotional. And nothing stirs emotion like a great story.

As people, we struggle to remember facts and figures, but we remember and retell stories quite easily. We pass these on from generation to generation because of how the story makes us feel. In true cinematic fashion, any great story will ring true to your client because it aligns with how they see themselves in the world. There is a subtlety involved that earns you their trust as the storyteller. The goal is to craft your message and marketing in a way that makes an exceptional promise and puts you in a position to fill it will appeal to the right client, at the right time.

A world view is not who you are. It's what you believe. It's your biases. A world view is not forever. It is simply what the consumer believes right now.

Much has been written about storytelling as a marketing tool, and I encourage you to look at authors such as Donald Miller and Seth Godin for in-depth education about creating marketing efforts and storytelling techniques. For now, let's go through the some of the basics.

First, you need to understand that this story is not, for, or about you. Ego-driven marketing efforts will always fall flat, because they appear to be preachy and they don't invite your clients to imagine themselves in your business. "About

Me" marketing leaves out your client, and therefore fails to connect at an emotional level.

Instead, begin with the client profile that you developed in Chapter 2. Imagine your client as the main character of your story. Think about who they are, and what their story is about.

What is the problem that they have that has brought them to your business? What is your main character's need, want, and fear? It may feel strange to think about hosting a wedding as a problem. If you find yourself struggling in that respect, ask yourself instead what it is that they need. The answer is never as simple as it appears.

People don't buy things, they buy feelings. When you position yourself as a person who sells stuff, you become a commodity. A commodity is easily replicated, undercut, and interchangeable with every other product or service in the market that does what you do on the surface. In the end, a client will always care less about the stuff and more about how the stuff makes them feel. As a business, we want our messaging to create the feelings that our clients wish to have, and we want that feeling to be really unique so that it cannot be found with any of our competitors.

Think of it this way; you are a great photographer and you're selling eight hours of wedding day coverage, plus an engagement session, and an album. Regardless of your style and scale, I guarantee you that every other wedding photographer in the world is selling the same thing on some level. In that respect, your competition can always outsell you. They can always add more hours to their coverage, add a second or third shooter, undercut your pricing, and throw in an extra print in order to secure the business. Imagine instead that your marketing speaks less about the amount of time that you spend at the wedding and more about your desire to capture the intimate moments of the day. You talk about the value of the engagement session as an opportunity for you to get to know your couple so that on the wedding day you feel like a friend and not just a stranger. You focus on how important it is that you design an album that provides complete coverage of all the little moments, from getting ready to their final send off, with every detail captured in a way that is guaranteed to look good fifty years from now. Do you see the difference? The first package is stuff. The second story is about emotion.

Once you understand your main character and what it is that they want from the process, you want to talk about what it is that they need to do. Any issue that they have will lead to steps that they can take to overcome it. For example, a couple has ten empty tables they need to fill. But what they really want to do is to create an environment that allows their guests to communicate with one another while also showcasing the menu that they have painstakingly selected. To do this, they need to hire a florist and event designer. They can't just choose anyone, they need to find someone who specializes in creating what they want. A number of obstacles will stand in their way. Everything from price point to style, availability, and season can impact a client's buying decisions. Ask yourself, what it is that you do, and how it is that you do it? Apply your skills to the goals that your client have. Do you source your flowers from around the club, making it possible to have nearly any bloom that they want regardless of season? Do you only work with local growers, because you care about giving back and you know that this type of farming is sustainable?

As you imagine your clients problems and needs, and you understand the obstacles that they have, you can begin to introduce yourself as their mentor and guide throughout the process. Think about what it is that you bring to their experience and how it aligns with their world view. Make a list of your very specific gifts and talents. Note how they make your client feel. Think about what it is that you do to create an emotion and a connection beyond the one thing that you are hired for.

The story of your business should take your clients on a journey. All of your marketing and content creation, from your blog to your social media and your in-person meetings and phone calls should be designed to take your clients on a journey. How does your business help them, specifically? What do you do that makes them feel special and unique? What skill set can you deploy that will help them sidestep problems and avoid mistakes? In what ways are you the only person that they can choose?

In closing out your story, you should always help your clients imagine the success that they will have at the end of the process. Describe how your couples will feel when they walk in to a room that has been beautifully decorated for them. Talk about the way that their guests will rave about the meal that your team of chefs has prepared. Take them further into their history, and talk about the value that that wedding album will have fifteen years from now not only to them, but to their future children.

Storytelling to your clients does not happen once. This is not just a page on your website or promotional piece of literature. Storytelling happens daily, with every post and touch point.

There are four different types of statements you can make in storytelling. They are:

Customer Focus Statements

Strategy Statements

Solution Statements

Critical Assumptions

A Customer Focus Statement is something that speaks directly about how your business will serve your ideal client. For example, my Customer Focus Statement is:

I exist to create extraordinary experiences for extraordinary people.

While the statement starts with I, it is really about what I do for the people that hire me. It's about them. My clients all lead extraordinary lives, and in many ways they are exceptional. This statement tells them that I understand how special they are, and the goal of my business is to give them something even better and more extraordinary than the things they get to experience on any regular day.

A Strategy Statement is not intended to be a list of things that you do. You're not outlining a set of tasks, or a specific pathway forward. Instead, you want to talk about the theory behind your business and how it supports your initial customer statement. My Strategy Statement is:

> I do this by bending the universe to my will, creating the perfect environment for those who value atmosphere and aesthetics.

Notice how the strategy behind my work supports the customer focus statement that I wrote previously. I am telling my clients what I intend to do, but not how I do it. It creates both a sense of trust, and a sense of mystery which is what allows me to be the expert in the story.

Next, create a Solution Statement. Knowing that your clients have needs and wants, you need to showcase your solution to their problems. For me, that means:

> Rather than look for perfection in an imperfect world, I create the world you wish you lived in. I import your desires onto a blank canvas.

What exactly did I say in the above statement? First, I'm acknowledging the fact that the world is not a perfect place, which makes my clients feel better about the fact that they have an issue. Every client I have ever had experiences some level of imperfection in their life. I bet that yours do, too. Some of them have family issues, others have financial issues, while others have experienced loss and heartache. By analyzing the imperfections, I open the door and give my clients permission to share those issues with me. I also demonstrate that I have a solution and a way through those issues. I let them know that their desires become mine, that I will create them in anyway that I need to, and that on their wedding day the world will feel like a perfect place for them in that moment.

The last and final statement that you will make is the Critical Assumption. This is the thing that you believe in above all else, and that your client must also believe in order for the two of you to work well together.

In my business that statement is:

The grander the moment, the better the memory.

I am somebody who believes that more is more, and that bigger is better. I prefer to add rather than remove, and I value over the top experiences because I believe that they create longer lasting memories. If a client does not believe that at their core, then I am not the right planner or designer for them. Attracting anyone who believes anything else will be a problem for my business and only leads to issues and failure for both myself and the client.

Having read through my example, take a moment to create your Four Core Statements. Write them out, and use them as the guiding principle for every blog post, social media message, and ad that you run.

Please remember, that these four statements will exist for every business, in every market segment. Whether your stationery business is new and just getting off the ground, or if you own a hair and make up company with twenty artists that have been servicing the industry for seven years, these statements are both implied and overt. They will guide your efforts in communicating who you are, who you are for, and why.

We are going to end this chapter with a challenge. I would like you to write all four statements, without referencing what it is that you do in the industry. Do not allow yourself to focus on the stuff. Focus only on the feelings that the stuff creates. Then, share the statements on social, tag me, and I will repost and share the best examples with my followers online.

PRESS AND PUBLISHING

Now that you have the right team members in place and you are telling the right story, it is time to begin operating as your own PR agency. Focus on the 3 P's: press, publication, and public relations.

PRESS

When it comes to pitching press opportunities, the most important thing is that you make it easy for reporters and bloggers to write about you. One of the easiest things you can do to begin manifesting press is simply to keep a press page on your site. This space should include your biography, a company description, and links to what you consider to be your best work. List out the topics on which you consider yourself to be an expert. Before you tell me - or worse, yourself - that you aren't an expert, acknowledge the skill and the talent that it takes to launch and run your own business. You have seen and done things that other people can learn about. Use your experience to your advantage.

Once your press page is established, create a list of local shows, newspapers, and magazines that you would like to be featured in. Research the writers and create a list of contacts that you can cold call or send an email to. Cold calling may seem old fashioned, but if you present yourself as a resource that can help the reporter, and if you provide them with a clear, organized pitch, you will find that many sources will respond favorably.

When dealing with the press, remember to approach this as a long-term relationship. Think beyond the scope of weddings and expand your reach by applying your expertise to lifestyle events. Lifestyle stories and articles are often planned in advance, and certain topics can be predicted with great accuracy. For example, the holidays happen at the same time every year, which allows you to pitch yourself as an expert in taking holiday photos or planning a holiday play list well in advance. The same is true for summer vacations, Halloween, spring break, etc.

Create a pitch for upcoming events and submit them two to three months in advance. You can build your own press calendar by listing all major national holidays and events, and then look up locally driven events on your city's event calendar.

In addition to pitching story ideas, you can also publish your own press release. Create a master press release form, and update it monthly. Use your press release to announce new products and services, spotlight special events, and make announcements. Once you finish your release, post and distribute it yourself on sites such as PR Web (www.prweb.com) and the PR Newswire (www.prnewswire.com).

PUBLICATION

One of the fastest and most effective ways to redefine your business and help raise the profile of your market is to get your weddings featured on blogs and in magazines.

Begin your publishing efforts with local blogs and magazines. Connect with your partners and agree to share the weddings you create together with a series of real wedding blogs. Agree that you will not only give one another credit, but that you will include live links to all of the vendor pages. By including all of the company names and websites, you are strengthening one another's search-ability via back links online.

Once you have gotten comfortable sharing your work in your own network, you want to move into actually submitting to standalone blogs, magazines, and publications. As traditional media changes, and social media continues to move to the forefront, being published and endorsed by a third-party arbiter of Style becomes more difficult simply because there are fewer publications available. It is for this reason that crafting a proper submission is so vital to your success. More often than not, it is the planner or the photographer that is charged with creating the submission, but anyone can submit work, both real weddings and styled shoots, for publication. To avoid confusion, it's best for the team to get together in advance and decide who will submit the work, and how.

When working with creatives that are struggling to be published, one of the biggest mistakes I see them making is that they wait until after the wedding to begin crafting their submission. As the team leader producing the event, you know better than anyone and well in advance what is going to be happening at a wedding. Rather than wait until the photos and video come in, craft your submission while you work on the timeline. This will help ensure that you don't miss any of the major details, and the energy and excitement will be fresh in your mind while you're pulling together the details.

Begin your submission by creating a full list of all vendors that are working on the wedding. You want to make sure that you have the company name, the name of the main contact and the coordinating phone number, email address, website, and social media handles included. A spreadsheet is the easiest way to organize this information.

Next, begin drafting the narrative of the day. You want to make it easy for an editor or a writer to say yes to your submission. Begin with a little bit of back story about your couple and include their names, how they met, and how they fell in love. Then, you can briefly touch on anything interesting that came up during the planning and design process. You want your story to have an arc and a hook that engages readers, so anything that your couple was really focused on, their priorities, and any challenges that were overcome make for a great story. Finally, write the story of the day as if it's already happened. Take time to imagine what both of the couple and the guests will experience at the wedding. All of the details should be top of mind, and so your ability to describe the colors and the flowers at the ceremony, the reception, the music and the menu should be very easy. Finally, draw up a shot list for your photography and video teams that corresponds with the story that you just wrote. Ask your photographers if these images can be edited and sent to you first, so that the submission can be sent in as quickly as possible.

This is a great exercise for a few reasons. It allows you to mentally walk through the day and identify any potential pain points and problems. You'll be able to run through the experience with the entire team, and with your clients. If anything is missing, or if something needs to be changed, you will be able to address those issues in advance rather than wait until you're on site and live.

In your submission, take special note of anything interesting that happens on site. I always begin a note in my phone at the start of a wedding. As the day moves on, I'll open it up and jot down anything that is incredibly emotional or funny that happens throughout the day. If my clients or partners say anything interesting, I add that in, as well. Then, once the photos are ready I am able to add in real facts and reactions from the wedding to make my submission as authentic as possible.

Many of us struggle with what to submit to an editor. I know that in the beginning of my career, my submissions were littered with photos of my couples and their guests. It made sense in my mind to focus on the newlyweds, and the fact that I had such an emotional connection to them made it hard to limit the images that I wanted to share. Working with a team of independent editors helped me craft a better submission and understand that while publications and future couples want to see two people in love, but they really want to see are the details. To ensure that I never miss a step, I created a submission check list. This list is sent to the photographer along with the shot list, and is my guide while culling images for editors.

A service such as Two Bright Lights will allow you to craft your submission once, and then submit to multiple platforms at one time. This is a great way to expose your work to a number of editors, and cuts down on your administration time.

Still, nothing takes the place or is as valuable as having an actual relationship with a real wedding Saturday. One of the best ways to develop these relationships is to meet editors face-to-face at conferences and industry events. If you have not had that opportunity however, you can work to develop relationships online. Do some digging and find out who the main contacts at your favorite publications are, and send them a note saying hello. Then, follow up every four to six weeks with something that they may find interesting and helpful. Ask if there's any content that they are currently missing, and offer to create it via a styled shoot. Or better yet, work with a team of partners to come up with an idea and pitch it to a publication in advance.

This process will take longer and require more of a

commitment. It's easy to get lost in the digital shuffle, especially if you were targeting a well-respected and highly trafficked blog or magazine. Being diligent (but not annoying) while also seeking to give the editor of your choice massive value in advance will pay off, as long as you are willing to put in the time and play the long game.

Being published by third-party is cause for celebration!

Be certain to re-post any images that a blog shares online, and share the link yourself across all of your social networks. Tag your publisher and show them how much you appreciate having your work included in their space. Blog about the submission process, share the final future, and be certain to include all credits so that the entire team can enjoy the benefits of being published.

PRESS PITCH CALENDAR

IN THIS MONTH	SUBMIT FOR	ON THESE TOPICS
January	April	Easter Passover Spring Weddings Spring Break
February	May	Kentucky Derby National Pet Month
March	June	Summer Weddings LGBTQ+ Pride
April	July	4th of July Ice Cream Month
May	August	End of Summer Parties Football
June	September	Fall Wedding Ideas

PRESS PITCH CALENDAR

IN THIS MONTH	SUBMIT FOR	ON THESE TOPICS
July	October	Halloween Party Ideas Black History Month
August	November	Men's Health Month Thanksgiving
September	December	Christmas Hanukkah New Year's Eve
October	January	New Year Tips and Tricks Organization
November	February	Valentine's Day Proposals
December	March	Spring Weddings Spring Cleaning

THE CREATORS STUDIO

Whether you are a new wedding professional that is just entering the space or a seasoned veteran, there is a thread of creativity that runs through the vein of your work. You must be able to see things that others do not see, and bring them forth into the world. Some days, it feels easy; you are a live wire of creative energy. On other days, you may just be… blank. There is a void, a dryness that cannot seem to be tapped into.

It is easy to be jaded and develop a "been there, done that" attitude. When faced with these feelings, those just in it to check boxes and turn out mass amounts of work are drawn to simply knocking off whatever feels the most relevant in the moment. How many times have you seen an extraordinary photo on Pinterest only to see it replicated (i.e., ripped off) quickly and often? Suddenly, you are no longer inspired, but annoyed.

This behavior is death to our industry. If all we need to do is copy what's been done, the what value do we bring to the table?

So then the question we all face is: "How do we maintain a constant source of creativity in an industry that creates sensory overload? How can we unblock ourselves and instead be fearless in putting something new out into the world?"

One of the things that I found to be so important in terms of fostering creativity is blocking out time to be creative. There is this myth that creativity is something that just happens; a spark out of nowhere. In reality, you can work on creativity. There are many books and workshops that teach ways in which to stimulate ideas. Every suggestion and method is valid, and you'll need to explore a few before finding the method that works best for you.

Schedule time in your week to work on creativity. Begin by thinking about when and where you work best. Creating the right environment that allows you to relax and pull out ideas is also helpful. Whether that means finding a place with complete silence or setting the scene with background music, again you need to find what works best for you. Next, settle in and get comfortable with something to write on and something to write with. While I am personally prone to using pen, I have a friend who finds colored pencils really inspiring. Write the topic that you want to work on across the top, and then brainstorm. Write down anything and everything that comes to mind. Do not judge yourself, and do not put any limits on what you can write. Let your mind wander, allow yourself to think of anything it wants, even if it is off topic. And then....Leave it.

Take a break from the list and do something else. Stand up, stretch, get a up of coffee, or take a quick walk. You'll be in the zone, and you want to break out of it. Get out of your head so that you can start again with a clean slate. When you are ready, return to the work you did and focus on whatever stands out to you. Your brain will start to make connections and you'll be able to extrapolate an idea, taking it further by adding to it with each creative session that you have.

Curiosity is one of the greatest sources of innovation. By seeking out new information in your field, or even learning about one of your partner's businesses, you'll be to create new synapses and connections in your brain. Those will help you see things differently, and encourage you to see things from a different angle. Many people in our industry look to fashion shows in Europe for inspiration. What the designers are doing in their collections will eventually find its way into bridal shops. Noting shapes, colors, and textures will put you at the forefront of what is coming before other industry pros have it on their radar.

Another great indicator of what will be happening in weddings and event design over the next twelve to twenty-four months is architecture and home decor. Looking at furniture, room layouts, and lighting is a great way to spot emerging event trends. Nature, as always, provides us with countless examples of inspiration and has been at the heart of many a design. Beyond simply looking at design magazines, I enjoy going and visiting new homes and construction communities. As an exercise, go to a new development and take a tour. Pay careful attention to the art that's hanging on the walls, the music that is being played in the background, and the way you feel while sitting in a space. Note three of your favorite things, and then imagine incorporating them into a wedding. Perhaps you will find a photo framed in a mock master bedroom that inspires a couple's portrait, or you hear a melody that could be perfect for guest seating music.

Don't be afraid to explore less popular avenues for inspiration. As the mother of two young children, I often find that there is a movie, cartoon, or game playing on repeat in my house. It's easy to drown that out and dismiss it as child's play. Instead, one day I took the opportunity to watch a movie with my kids, and found myself mesmerized by the costumes and live action telling of an old story. The sets were so elaborate, and the suspension of disbelief was so real that I began pulling elements in to a cocktail party that I was designing for an industry event. What originally was going to be a fairly straightforward and pretty function for 600 wedding professionals turned into a dark and mysterious woodland setting with fantastic creatures and fairy nymphs. The hook of a popular song, can serve as the same inspiration.

Many people advocate walking for fifteen to thirty minutes each day. I have a dog, and so walks are a very regular part of our routine. But walking for creativity means that you need to walk without distraction. No checking emails, no responding to text messages. You want to map your route and then walk in awareness. Take in your surroundings, let your mind wander, and pay attention to your thoughts. Some people carry a small notebook, and they take notes as they go. Personally, I don't. These are quick walks, and as soon as I walk in the door I jot down whatever came to me.

Some ideas take years to fully develop. Create a folder of the work you wish you were doing. We did this in the catering world all the time. It would start with an idea; such as an Italian market feast. We would work on a story and a narrative that would support the overall vision, and then develop a menu that we wanted to serve. Over time, we would revisit the ideas again and again, adding inspirational images, playing with the names of dishes, and discussing the interesting ways we could display the food. The more we worked on the development of the idea, the more real it became. We would mentally run through the menu and the event over and over again until we were comfortable knowing that we had a viable option that we could produce and sell. Then, we simply held it in a file that said "custom menus" and waited for the right client to come along. Once that client presented themselves, we would personalize the offering and pitch the menu to them as something that we wrote specifically in their honor. And in many ways, we did. We just didn't know them yet.

This is a practice all segments of the wedding and event industry can master. Whether it is an entertainment company working on a set list, a designer creating a table-scape, a photographer planning for a shoot in a special location, or a video team building out the storyboard for a film sometimes it is best to create the framework for your art, and then wait for the client to arrive.

Having these designs, ideas, or shots in your portfolio will serve you in a few ways. First, you allow yourself the opportunity to fully develop and explore your idea without the pressure of time constraints or client needs. Once you are confident in your overall design, you can practice your pitch and refine the offering. When the appropriate client does arrive at your door, you will have lived with the idea for so long that it will be real to you, allowing you to be confident in what you are selling, how you want to present it, and how you plan to execute it.

I personally have held back ideas for years. In early 2019 I produced an emerald green wedding that was inspired by The City of Oz. I had been working on this design for five years before it came to life. Was it easy to wait that long? No, not at all! But I knew that I needed the ideal combination of the right clients, in the right space, and with the right creative partners in order to do the idea justice. The waiting was terrible, but the satisfaction of seeing a thought come to fruition after all that time was extraordinary.

Should you find that patience is not your greatest virtue, and if you absolutely must get the idea out of your head now, you can always present the idea to your partners and build a styled shoot around it. How long you should wait is completely at your discretion. If your business does a lot of volume, I would say that you can hold back for six to twelve months. If your business is more boutique and you manage fewer clients, then I would suggest holding back for anywhere from one to three years. In my experience, it is always more satisfying to bring a thought to life for real couples than it is to minimize the design in a styled shoot, but I leave that to you.

Whether produced for the community, for clients, or just for yourself the goal is to constantly develop the art of creatively. Creativity is a practice not unlike yoga. Experiment with a number of different techniques until you find the one that works for you, schedule time for creative pursuits each week, and build upon your ideas until they become viable experiences.

CONTENT CREATION

As wedding professionals, we are responsible for communicating with both clients and colleagues. In a world that makes it easy to re-post, re-tweet, and re-gram from other members of our community, the key to your true value lies in creating original content that supports your four statements and tells your story.

Original content is exactly what it sounds like: original content. This means that it is content created by your business, with a team of partners, that exists solely to move your business forward and to speak to your future clients and the community. I've heard wedding pros talk about how blogging is dead, or that social media doesn't matter. Every time I hear someone say this, I want to scream! Social media is the contemporary cocktail party. It's where our clients and our colleagues are hanging out. This is where they discover our businesses, where they learn about us as individuals, and where they seek confirmation about who we are and what we do.

I cannot say that strongly enough. If you fail to create original content with specific messaging, and if you don't spend time developing a social media strategy, then your business is utterly irrelevant and will at some point cease to exist. Social media is the new town hall, it's the town crier, more valuable than a recommendation from someone's mother's cousin, and the currency is greater than any ad dollars you have to spend.

There are four ways in which our customers and the industry consume content. They Read, they Look, they Listen, and they Watch.

READ

Blogging is the grandfather of all content creation. While currently out of fashion as many people prefer social media, blogging is not by any means dead. Businesses that blog consistently benefit in a number of ways. First, there is nothing better than blogging to create a strong SEO campaign. Writing blogs allows you to speak about the topics, clients, and trends that matter to your business. By doing this, your website becomes more searchable, and is crawled more often by sites such as Google, Yahoo, and Bing. All of the major search engines prioritize websites that are updated and a regular basis, meaning that blogging will help your site rank higher than any other cost-free activity you can engage in.

Much has been said about SEO (search engine optimization) and the things you should and should not do with regard to do blogging. Algorithms seem to change every single day, and so my personal belief is that you should write about the things you want to write about, and that you share your point of view in a way that feels natural and authentic to you. That said, there are a few things you should be aware of. First, aim for a word count of 300 - 500 words per blog. This will ensure that the search engines actually have something to search! When adding in photos or video, be certain to include credits and a full description of the image. You can use both the caption and the meta data to do this. Also, please be sure to check the size of the photos and video to ensure that they do not slow the loading of your page. Adding a full list of credits to your blog is also important. It shows support for your industry partners and generates good will. Plus, the likelihood of another vendor sharing what you publish is more likely if you have credited their work.

Industry partners are not the only people who can share your work, however don't forget to add social sharing buttons. Always make it easy for readers to share your work to sites such as Facebook, Twitter, Pinterest, LinkedIn, and more. Don't be afraid to ask people to share! A call to action is vital. Add a note at the top of the blog, or close out your writing with a simple request to the reader.

More important to me, however, is the platform that blogging provides you with. When you post to social media, you do not own that content, nor do you own the link that is attached to it. You are limited in size and scope, and what you put out today can disappear tomorrow if a platform falls out of favor. Remember when there was a chance that Style Me Pretty was going to shutter and everyone lost their minds? Why were they so worried? Well, first and foremost, Style Me Pretty is a beloved arbiter in our industry, and as such both couples and wedding pros had a deep affection and connection to the brand. On a much more selfish level, however, the industry was deeply concerned about links to their work, galleries, and showcasing their business.

While ownership of Style Me Pretty was, thankfully, taken back by the original founders and continues to thrive, the potential closure serves as a lesson to all of us. Create, post, and manage your own blog. It is the only way to ensure that your content is yours, that it will last, and that it will always be available online.

Be certain that your website and your blog has a copyright on it. It's easier than ever to "borrow" (i.e., steal) from one another online. While I know that you would not do that, I would hate to see you be the victim of such disrespectful and unscrupulous behavior. Protect your content and safeguard your work by simply adding the copyright symbol © and the dates of operation to every page of your website.

Beyond blogging, your clients are also reading articles. While I always support efforts to have your thoughts published in magazines and on industry blogs, I highly recommend re-purposing a portion of your original article on LinkedIn. Who's reading LinkedIn looking for a wedding photographer, or a florist? You would be surprised!

I always considered LinkedIn to be the Facebook of the business community, and while the platform has certainly become more social over the last few years, it remains a strong hold for professional connections and relationship building. The trick to successfully using LinkedIn is to know your audience and speak to their needs.

Why are you on LinkedIn? The answer is likely to create business connects and opportunities. Now apply that to the audience. If you are a venue, you can use LinkedIn to connect with photographers whose work you admire. If you are a florist, you may be able to attract the attention of a wedding planner or venue that needs someone to refer business to. LinkedIn will allow you to post jobs, ask questions, and see what other members of the industry need. Knowing what your colleagues are looking for will put you in a unique position to fill the gap, making you and your business valuable to them as people.

LinkedIn is also the first place professionals go to update their job status. Imagine seeing that a venue manager you have wanted to work with has changed jobs and has a new position at another location. You see it on LinkedIn, research the address of his or her new employer, and you send a hand written card congratulating them on their new home. Imagine how surprised that venue manager would be, and how high on their radar you would be.

LOOK

It seems like scrolling is everyone's favorite pastime. We scroll through Instagram, we scroll through Facebook, we scroll, scroll, scroll. As our attention span get shorter, and our fingers move faster, the ability to catch someone's attention is going to depend more on the visuals and images we put in front of them. It's for this reason, that photography is so important. As a wedding planner, I am always looking for photographers who capture the world in the same way that I, and my clients, see it. A quality image can make an entry-level wedding look extraordinary, while one bad angle or overly exposed shot can degrade the work of everybody involved.

Platforms like Instagram, Facebook, and Tumblr are driven by the imagery. When posting to these platforms, every image should be a hero shot. The photo should be strong enough to stop someone from scrolling and inspire them to go back. Vertical images that take up the most space will inspire greater engagement simply by virtue of the fact that they are larger and command more attention. However, a strong landscape image or square cropped photo will always stand out.

Unless you were a photographer, your ability to create a somewhat cohesive look on visual platforms can be difficult. It's likely that the events you work on are being shot by a number of photographers from across the country. If that's the case, you need to be even more diligent as you select what photos you will post.

First, look for photos that properly showcase your contribution to the wedding. Yes, your job is to tell your client's story and to speak to future couples that may be a good fit for your business. The best way to do that, is to show something that you have done that led to a beautiful and successful wedding for your past clients. If you're a band or DJ, images of a packed dance floor are always great to share. Invite the photographer up onto stage, or behind the DJ booth so they can get the best image. For florists and rental companies, you want to share a mix of empty room detail shots and images of people enjoying the atmosphere that you created. Stationary and invitation companies, of course, will show the finished product that they create for their clients, but I also encourage them to share room shots, images of the couples, and coordinating details. The goal is to showcase the kinds of couples that you work with, and the type of wedding your products support. Dress salons, stylists, beauty experts, and accessory companies can follow the same line of advice. Focus on showing your contribution to the overall wedding, while also sharing overall images that set the tone and identify who your ideal client is.

Next, you want to look at the overall feel of the images that you're posting. If you have consistently shared light images that are bright and airy, but your most recent wedding is darker, break up your posting and help transition from one style to another by posting a quote or adding a black and white image to the mix.
Lastly, encourage other wedding professionals and former clients to share your work by giving them credit.

You obviously want to tag the photographer, but I'm sure that you are also giving a little bit of social love to the other vendors and partners that made the day such a success. I always appreciate it when another industry professional shares my work, and seeing them re-post and share something that I've created exposes me to a whole new group of potential clients and professionals that may not have seen me otherwise.

Use your posted image to attract attention, and then support it by adding meaningful captions. I don't advocate click bait; that is, where you post an image that you know will get someone's attention but that doesn't match the messaging or your brand. Instead, use whatever image you post as the open door that allows you to discuss something important to you. For example, let's say you have a standing room shot that looks like absolute perfection, but you know that there are struggles and challenges behind the scenes. Post the image, and then use the caption to discuss how important it is to have strong partnerships that you can rely on during a wedding load in. Before and after images, especially for hair and make up and always with someone's permission, are amazing and will give you an opportunity to discuss airbrushing versus traditional make up application. A photo of a towering cake with lots of layers and sugar flowers is a great opportunity for you to talk about labor charges and the amount of time it takes to construct such a masterpiece.

Never underestimate a call to action in a caption. A beautiful image is a great opportunity for you to ask a question of your followers. Questions boost engagement as they inspire people to get involved with your business. They let your followers know that you care about what they think, and the answers will provide valuable feedback into what matters most to the people who engage with your business. You may also suggest that your followers check out a new blog post or podcast, pointing them to another channel of yours that they can support. You can take a poll,

61

offer of a challenge, or simply ask them to drop an emoji in the comment section.

One final word on images. In a highly curated society where we all focus on the pretty and the perfect, a solid picture taken with your own phone that shows something behind the scenes or as it happens will always generate attention. If you really want to stand out in a sea of professional images on social, learn to take a decent picture yourself and share it in the moment. I don't know how they do it, but sites like Instagram and Facebook can tell when you post an organic image. Your social media channels will reward you for it by making the photo more visible and by putting your business in front of more people.

LISTEN

When I was a kid, we listened to the radio. It was on in the car, in the house, and on my Walkman. We carried around in boxes, idolized D.J.'s, and talked about interviews with our favorite celebrities and other call-in listeners.

The podcast is today's version of talk radio. As a wedding professional, if you are just starting out or if you've been in the industry for many years, you have a voice and a perspective. With that voice comes responsibility to use it. No other medium gives you as great of an opportunity to just talk about the things that matter to you. And let's be honest, while some of us may struggle to write or to create a pretty picture, we all know how to talk.

Starting a podcast is intimidating for a number reasons.

First in for most, many people in our industry struggle to figure out what equipment they need, where they should host, and how they should publish. Let me clear that up right now in one quick and easy word: Anchor. The Anchor app is free and will download directly to your phone, with other versions available for your tablet and your desktop. Starting a podcast with Anchor is easy. You simply download Anchor, name your show, hit a button and begin recording. When you're done, and Anchor will push out your episode across multiple platforms, making it easy for listeners to find you on iTunes, Stitcher, Spotify, etc.

When you start your podcast, think about the listener first. Are you trying to attract the attention of other industry professionals in an effort to establish yourself as an expert? Or is this for potential clients who are looking for tips and tricks when it comes to hiring someone in your profession? As with all efforts in marketing, it starts with knowing who your audience is and what type of content will resonate with them.

Next, make a list of all of the topics you feel are relevant to your listeners and that you are comfortable discussing as an expert. Not comfortable talking about a certain topic? Draw a line away from that topic and make a list of people that are experts that you can invite on a special guests.

Being asked to be a guest on a podcast is an honor, and many will be flattered to be invited on your show. Once you confirm them as a guest, be sure to treat them as such! Make the experience easy for your guests by providing them with a lot of information. Information is power! Send an email in advance that explains the format you will be taping on, and advise your subject on whether you are taping audio, video, or both. Note in writing how you plan to use each medium, and give an overview of how you anticipate the interview going. I always like to ask if there are any questions or topics that my guest does or does not want to touch on. Recognize that this is a vulnerable space; make efforts to help put your guest at ease.

After the podcast is taped, be sure to send a Thank You note to your guest. Once the podcast is live, send another email sharing the link and the episode cover so that your guest can share it as well.

Once you have a list of topics and the guests you have to do the scary thing; which is begin taping. This is where you need to give yourself a little grace, and understand that you probably won't be the very best podcast host in the beginning. In fact, it's more than likely that you're going to be terrible. Embrace it! Start out by letting your listeners know that this is scary and new to you. Be vulnerable and share with them why you've started this podcast, and what it is that you hope to get from it. Take them behind the curtain and be real and raw so they can see who you are.

So many people use social media like a megaphone, just ranting at the void, filling the space with their words. There is a lot of posturing online, and clients can sense that a mile away. Go against the grain by standing firmly in your place and embrace who you are and where your business is. Talk about your successes, your challenges, and your fears. Encourage people to write in with questions that you can answer, and invite people who believe differently than you on to create a lively but respectful debate. Understand that this is an opportunity to create conversation. There's a conversation that you have with your listener which, while one-sided, is important as it allows someone to get to know you. There is the conversation that takes place with guests that can educate your listeners, and there are call-in opportunities with live broadcasts that are always fun.

The most important thing is that you were talking to the people, and listening to how they respond.

WATCH

My youngest child encountered a commercial recently and was horrified to find out that we were forced to watch them "in the olden days". This is what digital media has done! And yet look at all of the opportunity it's created for people like us.

In my opinion, YouTube is like the Wild West of television. One-part network show, one-part cable, YouTube allows us all the opportunity to create our own channels and shows. If you thought podcasting was scary, just imagine getting in front of camera! Some of us are natural performers, and have no problem sitting in front of a camera or phone and taping a video. Others struggle, not quite knowing what to say, feeling awkward, and tensing up when the camera is placed in front of them.

The benefit of video is that it connects you to your audience in a way that no other medium does. When you post a video on YouTube, or if you go live on stories or Facebook, you give people an idea of who you are right in this moment. Your potential clients see how you move and carry yourself. They can hear the inflection of your voice, and note excitement, control, concern, and authority. Video creates an intimacy that closely mimics what someone would experience if they were in front of you. There's a trust that develops, as those watching begin to feel that they know you.

Approach your YouTube channel the same way that you approach your podcast. Determine in advance who the channel is for, and what is that day will get from watching an episode of your show. The goal is always to fill a void. Imagine every question that a potential client could possibly ask you, and then film yourself answering that question. Make a list of issues you've encountered as you've tried to do your job, and discuss the steps you've taken to move beyond them and be successful in your space. Use screen-sharing software to document how you organize your business and move about your day, and show people what it really takes to run your business.

I am a big believer in the idea that you cannot sell what you cannot show. It's for this reason that I began creating behind-the-scenes videos of the set up of my weddings. The truth is, it was my husband's idea. I had been working on what was (at the time) the largest and most elaborate wedding of my career, when my husband said, "I don't think anyone has any idea what it takes to pull off a wedding like this. You should make a video of what happens over the four days of this wedding." The idea was interesting to me.

Everyone knows what the end result looks like, they have all seen the pretty. And yet it's the process and how we all do what we do that clients are really paying for. What would happen if we recorded it all as it went down and cut it into a 10 minute clip? I found someone that I trusted, and we embarked on this project without really having any idea as to where it would go.

That video is what closes all of my new clients. They see me crawling on the floor, holding a crying baby, counting silverware, and walking my bride through the space. They can imagine themselves in the room with me, and have a first hand accounting of what I will do to make their wedding a success. This is more authentic than any styled shoot, and it shows the magnitude of the work that goes into one of my weddings.

Regardless of what segment of the market you work in, or what type of wedding you work on, I guarantee you that there is something interesting that happens behind the scenes that your future clients would love to see. Maybe it's packing up your gear to ensure that you're never without an extra battery, or the way that you process the stems of roses. It could be a band practice, or the way in which a DJ goes about creating a playlist. Their hair and makeup tutorials, discussions on different types of paper and materials that can be used for invitations, and chefs plating live during the wedding. Each one of us is an expert in our own business, and we are the only ones who can show who we are and how we work.

Beyond the traditional YouTube channel, we all have the ability to go live on social media. Clients today require a personal connection. They want to know us as people. Live video is the easiest way to let out potential clients get a glimpse of who we are in real life. The nice thing about Instagram Stories and Snapchat is the ephemeral quality that they have. Unlike your actual feed, which is static and lasting, a live posting is here today and gone tomorrow. This allows you to experiment with a lot of different places for filming, topics, and trends. You can flip on the camera and show everything from your workout to your favorite lunch spot. Share your family and friends, your vacation, your set-up, and your tear down. You don't need to be perfectly camera-ready with live videos. They are supposed to be raw and real. You can show off your personality with fun filters, and you can invite people to engage with you in the moment and immediately.

Currently, your live videos are search-able by hashtags. Play with the idea of having a member of your team showcase our wedding as it happens, do a live Q&A, or create short little vignettes that will entertain people and endear you to them.

Go back to the statements that we talked about in storytelling, and apply them to your video marketing efforts. Create one video that supports your clients statement, while another supports your critical assumption. Show people what matters to you, and why.

Come on, let's get social!

STRATEGY AND DISTRIBUTION

Creating original content that speaks to your ideal client isn't enough; you need to distribute that content in a way that makes sense.

I ask every wedding professional and business that I consult with what their social media strategy is. More often than not, the answer is something along the lines of "I post to Instagram twice a day," or "I plan to start a blog/podcast/ YouTube channel." While valiant and worthwhile efforts, neither of these is a social media strategy. Strategy involves much more than simply posting and crossing your fingers, hoping for a result.

A strategy is an actual plan with measurable results. In order to create a social media strategy, you will need to set goals for yourself, align those goals with the proper networks, and then measure your results against your efforts.

The first thing you'll need to do in developing a social media strategy is to set your goals. For some businesses, increasing brand awareness is a goal. This is important for newer companies, or businesses that have recently gone through a re-branding. Most businesses, wish to generate new leads. Leads convert to purchases and clients are the lifeblood of our business. Applying effective social media strategies in order to attract these clients should always be a level one priority. Other businesses may want to use one channel in order to boost support and awareness for another social media channel. For example, you may wish to use your Instagram account to create awareness for your podcast or YouTube.

Begin by listing one or two goals for yourself that are measurable and that can be achieved within a certain time frame. For example, you could say, "I want to increase brand awareness and attract 200 new followers to my Instagram in the next thirty days." Or, you could say something like, "I want to attract one new customer that is interested in my highest priced package through posts on Facebook."

The next thing you need to do is determine which social media channels will be best suited to help you reach your goals. As mentioned before, LinkedIn is the most professionally best social media network, and is a great place to focus your efforts if you were interested in creating more B2B opportunities. Pinterest however is still one of the leading channels for generating traffic to the website. Out of all of my followers and efforts and all of my social media channels, Pinterest is still the greatest traffic generator I have. A quick look at your website analytics should tell you where the most activity is coming from.

Those numbers will help you in determining where you'll get the most ROI for your efforts. Just a note here, the "I" here for "Investment" is not necessarily money, but actually your time/effort/energy. You only have so many hours in a day, so focus them on the platforms that provide the highest ROI for you.

Once you've determined your goals and decided where to focus your efforts, it's always smart to take a look at your competition. Identify three to five companies in your segment of the industry that you admire, and see if you can determine what their strategy is. Do they post on certain days, or at certain times? Do they seem to have a pattern in what they're showing? How have they used social media to position their business, and how many followers do they have? More important than followers is engagement. Anyone can buy followers today. When you look at your competition you also want to note how many comments they have, how many likes and follows they are getting, and how many views they have.

Once you have a clear understanding of your competition, you can make the decision to either be inspired by their strategy and adopt certain components as your own, or you may decide to be the "anti-" and set yourself apart by doing something completely opposite of what your closest competition is doing.

When it comes to marketing and business practices in

general, my personal inclination has always been to go left when everyone else is going right. However, there is something to be said for the basics. It's important to understand the rules and abide by them before you can break them. Along that line of thought, you'll want to do some of the basics and mimic tactics that work to establish your strategy and results when you first launch your strategy.

After you have established your goals, identified the social media networks that you want to focus on, and analyzed your competition, you are going to want to create a schedule for content. There are a lot of tech gurus out there trying to teach you how to set up your social media ones and then ignore it for the rest of the month. Personally, I cannot think of a worse approach to take! Social media needs to be current. It's a conversation, and that requires that you show up and put in the work every single day. Still, there's a good chance you're gonna wake up on certain days and not feel like it. You may not feel well and be sick, you may draw a blank, or you may be super slammed on another project and just want to phone it in really quickly. I've been there, I get it. And that's why having a strategy and a schedule is so important.

When you're setting up a schedule, the first thing you want to do is come up with a list of all the different types of content that you can post on a regular basis. I always recommend planning out your content in a way that is useful for the end-user. Your messaging and posts should be designed to delight and inspire your clients and educate your colleagues and the community.

Only after you've consistently delivered valuable and interesting content should you ever post anything that is sales-y. In other words, don't ask your followers to do anything such as repost or re-tweet, don't ask them to buy, and don't ask them for any type of testimonial until you have absolutely given them something that has added to their experience.

I've developed a list of over 500 topics for each category of our industry, and over 300 topics for small businesses. When working with clients to develop a social media strategy the first thing we do is sit down and brainstorm together. I ask them to start by making a list of what they believe their ideal clients and followers would be most interested in. Then, we break each one of those topics down further into more specific sub-items. For example, a wedding photographer may believe that his or her followers want to see photos of real weddings. Break down the real weddings into all of the items that a photographer may shoot; getting ready images, details, portraits, the ceremony, the reception, dances and toasts, and the after party. Now, we break down each of those further. How many items and moments could be photographed while the couple is getting ready? There's various stages of makeup, various stages of dresses, a bride or groom alone, and then surrounded by their family and friends. There could be times when someone is writing out their vows, or opening up their wedding gift. Maybe they are posing with jewelry, or there is a dress standing on its own. While developing your strategy, go through this process in every area of a wedding that you may touch. At first, the ideas should come to you very quickly and very easily. When you start slowing down and feel like maybe you've reached the end of the list, go back to the beginning and start breaking down each item further. It is not enough to say that you can post about the tablescape when you can, in fact, break that down to posts about chargers, custom flatware, gold-rimmed glasses, the value of mercury glass votive candles over milk glass, etc.

Once your list is complete, you may choose to lay it out on an actual calendar, or you can simply keep it as a note in your phone and cross off topics as you discuss them. The goal is to always have an idea on hand so that you were never without something to say.

As you begin to create content, you will find that your audience begins to engage with you. It is of the utmost importance that you engage back. Do you want to show appreciation to former clients who continue to support your business, while proving to potential future clients that you are an active and thoughtful member of the community? It's smart to check in on your last three posts several times a day. Look at the people who have liked it or shared it. Are there any names that you don't know? If so, check out their profile and maybe drop them a note thanking them for engaging with you. Respond to absolutely every comment that is left on one of your posts. And always make sure that you were responding to every email.

As your business attracts more attention and your social media strategy begins to pay off, it's easy to feel overwhelmed by the amount of activity that is taking place. Some platforms, such as Facebook and Instagram, are integrated and will keep all activities in one place.

However, you may want to consider a social media management platform. There are many options available on the market today, including Buffer, Later, and eClincher. Some of these programs are free, while others charge a fee. Explore all options until you find what's right for you.

Once you have a handle on the process of posting, responding, and engaging with your followers you will want to elevate your social strategy. It's time to begin promoting all of your content by using one social channel to drive traffic to another. There are a number of ways that you can do this. First, identify which channel gets the most engagement and set that as your baseline. Use that channel to create awareness of the other channels you currently have. For example, you can post about your Podcast with an Instagram post, or use Instagram Stories to drive traffic to your YouTube Channel. Create hero images that you can post to Pinterest that will drive your audience to a blog post, and refer to your Facebook Business Page or Industry Group on your Twitter account.

Upon creating the first round of original content, you will want to post it everywhere. The goal is to have every post on social media refer back to the original piece you created. Then, stagger a number of posts across various platforms that reference the original piece in different ways, at different time, and across multiple platforms. In a way, it's like ping pong. You create a piece of original content; a blog for example. Next, you distribute the blog across all major platforms: Facebook, Twitter, Instagram, LinkedIn, and Pinterest. Be sure to use different images and captions to differentiate your message so that it appeals to your ideal client across each platform. Watch your posts and content, and note the engagement across all channels. Respond to all comments, research new followers, and direct message new followers that you believe will become clients or colleagues.

While the creation of original content is intended to be ongoing, you should continue to link back to your original content over several days during the initial publication. Begin by posting repeatedly on social on the first day, especially on Twitter as the timeline tends to move very quickly. Then, stagger the posts with less frequency on days two and three. As new content emerges, your efforts will go to the new piece, naturally, leaving the older content to live on as a search-able, valuable part of your SEO history.

Every month, review your efforts and set them against your goals. How did you do? Did you gain the amount of followers you wanted to attract? You will want to re-purpose older pieces that did well. Change the caption or the lead in an attempt to attract new eyes.

Remember, as an industry our clients are created daily. New couples get engaged, begin wedding planning, and start searching for vendors every day. Imagine that you posted a beautiful wedding three days ago. Your ideal clients get engaged next week. What is the likelihood that he or she will see it? The only way to guarantee that your best work is constantly found is to re-purpose it and share it repeatedly.

The best way to ensure that you are sharing the right content at the right time is to create a schedule. Go back to the list

CONFERENCES
& CONNECTIONS

Once you have established roots in your local community, it is imperative that you seek connections on a national level. When you are operating in local market, there is a tendency to get tunnel vision in terms of the gaps that exist today. In order to truly redefine your business, and your market, you must look beyond your front door and engage with wedding professionals that have a broader view of the industry and the world.

Attending nationally recognized conferences that attract wedding professionals from all across the world is the first step in broadening your view. For me, attending the Engage! Luxury Wedding Summit was instrumental in broadening my view. Engage! was scheduled to take place in Las Vegas within months of launching my business. Money was tight, and I didn't know if I could afford to attend or if there was enough value. My husband insisted I go, and the long term effects of being a part of the Engage! family have been tremendous. I was put in a room with the titans of our industry, I listened to planners, designers, photographers, and entertainers from around the world talk about their path and the struggles and successes that they had achieved. I sat with motivational speakers and business strategists, and when I returned home after my first day my head was spinning!

Two things stuck me deeply after my first day in session. The first, was that this was a viable business, and that there were a large number of people out there creating the kind of work that I wanted to do, and that they were enjoying a level of success that I had not thought possible. The second thought, sadly but honestly, was that I wasn't there yet. I actually remember saying to my husband, "I don't have a right to be in this room; I have nothing to offer these people!" His response was that I may not be on their level yet, but that if I continued to work and show up, if I attended the lessons, met people, and learned, that someday I would be.

Years later I am proud to say that I am a part of the Engage! family. I have been lucky to travel the world with this conference both as an attendee and as a speaker. Some of the most important and authentic relationships I have today are #becauseofengage. (If you are not familiar with that hashtag, plug it into Instagram, Facebook, and Twitter. You will be amazed at what pops up!)

Beyond Engage, there are a number of other conferences and organizations that are consistently hosting mixers and educational opportunities. The Knot Worldwide travels around the country putting on seminars taught by educators from around the globe. NACE (National Association of Catering and Events), The Special Event Show, and WIPA (Wedding International Professional Association) all offer opportunities for wedding professionals to learn from one another and other members of the hospitality community. Other conferences, such as WPPI (Wedding and Portrait Photography International), CaterSource, and the DJ Collective produce events that are more specialized for specific segments of the industry. Those searching for education and connection in the destination world can find a home with IADWP (International Association of Destination Wedding Professionals) and EPIC (Event Planners International Collaborative) founded by Marcy Blum and Sarah Hayward.

Why is this valuable to you? Because growth happens outside of your comfort zone. By attending conferences that bring together though leaders from other markets you will be exposed to incredible education and inspiration. Messages are delivered by iconic industry leaders that are not only standing on stage and speaking, but working in the industry as active members of our community.

As important as the education is, the real value of these conferences comes from the connections you will make and the relationships you build. Set your ego aside, and accept that we all want to grow and be better at what we do. While you are at a conference, look for people who are doing to type of work that you want to do, and see if you can connect with them on a personal level. Start small, one on one, and allow time for the relationship to build. As you attend a conference over and over again, you will begin to find your people, your tribe. Stay in touch on social media by actively liking, commenting, and sharing the work of those your admire. Then, once you feel the relationship taking form, feel free to reach out on email and text. Share information and books you think they may find interesting. Suggest that you meet in person when you are in their town. Make plans to connect when you attend the next conference.

You need to play the long game, and realize that these relationships can take years to develop. Don't give up, and don't be pushy. There is nothing worse than meeting someone for the first or second time, only to be hit with the "let's work together" email when you haven't cemented a real and authentic connection. You need to prove yourself valuable first, and then create opportunities to work together.

Here is a case study of something that actually happened:

During my second Engage! I met wedding photographer Dennis Kwan. Dennis is incredibly tall and eye catching, and for his first Engage! he was friendly and open, but also vulnerable and sweet. We sat together during a session and began following one another on social media.

Three years later, while producing a Wedding MBA event for The Knot, I was introduced to Cherish and Lindsay, the owners of Le Reve Films. We knew a lot of the same people and had a great time talking during the conference and afterwards at the party.

A month later, we were all in New York together for Bridal Fashion Week and The Knot Gala. Everyone got along and had a blast, and we continued to see one another, connect, and form solid relationships.

In the middle of all of this a mutual friend and wedding photographer, Brian Leahy, introduced me to an entertainer named Jordan Kahn of the Jordan Kahn Orchestra at a launch party for PartySlate in LA. Jordan invited us all to cocktails afterwards and surprised the entire group bu ordering pizza for everyone. Obviously, I was obsessed.

For the next three years - yes, THREE years - I watched all of these wedding professionals grow their businesses. I saw the commitment they had made to their education, and to giving back to the community. Their Instagram posts were always on brand, their work was spectacular, and I found that when we were together we all clicked. One night we were all talking and someone asked "Who is Elwynn and Cass? They have been blowing up my social!" We all agreed that this new company was making major moves on Instagram, and that their work as a Beauty Concierge was exquisite. The owner reached out to me about Engage! and signed up for the next conference.

I decided then and there that I wanted to work with all of these people. How could I not? They were friends, colleagues, and businesses that I admired. Each one was excelling in their own respective field, and I knew that we would have more power together than we did alone. Within three months I booked all of them, separately and together! I was able to book Brian Leahy and Jordan Kahn Orchestra for one wedding and Dennis Kwan, Le Reve Films, and Elwynn and Cass another. As a team, and with the support of some of my favorite local partners, we were all unstoppable. We all came from different cities, and we brought new perspectives and ideas to the table. Each of these weddings went on to be featured in national print publications, on blogs, and they all enjoy a certain amount of viral social media.

By dedicating the time and investing in education and relationships, each business was able to create something new that could not exist in their own local market. The work we did was strong enough to garner national attention, and it raised the profile of all of our businesses as a whole.

To achieve these results, here are the steps you will want to take:

1. Identify the conference(s) you feel most align with the business you want to do in the future.
2. Commit to attending the conference(s) at least once a year, every year, for a minimum of three years.
3. Identify the wedding professionals that you would like to connect with. You should plan to seek out two sets of people; one that you can learn from, and the other that you can grow with.
4. Be gracious and respectful to everyone, you never know who the person next to you is or will be.
5. Be interested in others, and interesting to those who speak to you.
6. Stay sober. Nothing will damage you more than embarrassing yourself at an industry function.
7. Take the education seriously! These conferences

look like a party, and they are, but you are there to learn! The only education that matters is the one you actually apply to your business and your market. I take two sets of notes when I attend a conference. The first set is session by session, notes that I can revisit and reread so that I can really absorb the information. The second set of notes is a quick list of actionable items that I can put in place within 48 hours of returning home that will immediately differentiate my business from my competition.

8. Send a Thank You note to the speakers who truly impacted you, and a nice to meet you note to anyone you felt a connection with.

9. Follow everyone you admire on social media. Actively engage with their businesses. Like, comment, and share the work that you admire. Leave notes on their blogs. Don't be creepy, but be supportive and real in your efforts to support their art.

10. If you have the opportunity to connect in person away from the conference take it! I cannot tell you how many events I've booked for people over lunch!

11. Year 2: Repeat. Dig deeper. Carve out time to spend with the people you truly want to get to know.

12. Year 3: Repeat again.

13. Create an opportunity for the people you want to work with to create something. Perhaps you are a DJ who wants to work with a planner. Suggest them as a speaker for a local conference. Or

if you are a florist that respects the work of a videographer, hire them to film a video series for your website.

14. Remember that nothing is owed to you; and the best way to create good will and meaningful relationships is to invest in the businesses you respect and admire.

15. Play the long game, and don't give up hope! I have a list of wedding pros that I am dying to work with, and in time I know I will.

Ultimately, developing national relationships will expose you to ideas and education that simply don't exist in your local market. By identifying trends and business processes that are not yet being executed where you live, you will can set your business apart and stand out in the saturated crowd. By elevating your business, you will have the opportunity to create real relationships with wedding professionals from other markets that share your beliefs and have the same level of education, and by pooling your resources you can do work that attracts attention on a national level, raising not only your profile, but the profile of the city you currently operate in.

CREATE YOUR COMPETITION

As your business grows and begins to attract more attention, you may find that you are being considered as the "only" for a certain segment of the population looking for your services. This can be exciting, and it certainly is flattering to be exhausted as the singular option for couples seeking what you do. You will be respected for the changes you have made, and many people may start to wonder what you are doing in XYZ town when your work has a more polished or elevated feel. This is when you know it's time to create your own competition.

It may sound crazy to think that you want to create another option for couples, when your goal is to grow your own business. This is the perfect time, however, to do just that. Look at markets outside of the wedding industry. There is Coca Cola and Pepsi, Apple and Microsoft, McDonald's and Burger King. One competitor legitimizes the other by virtue of the fact that they simply exist. One is no longer the outlier. By having a choice, the very work that you seek to do is normalized and accepted in your market.

The most important thing to realize at this stage is that you as a person and your creative business is not for everyone. As a creative business in the growth stage, your goal is to create a demand for a certain level of quality and experience. Once that demand is there, you must accept that you will not have the bandwidth to properly service each of the potential clients that come to you. As a person, you won't want to. This is about niche, being only for those who truly understand and respect what you do. Those people will change dates, shift locations, and compromise in various areas in order to have that which you provide. But what about the others? Clients that you perhaps do not have a connection with, or whom have booked a venue on a date where you are not available. You have a responsibility to them, and to your market, to provide them with an option that best meets their needs and that serves your community of local vendors as a whole.

Having done the work to create local relationships, you will easily be able to identify another business in your field that you respect and trust. You will likely also receive compliments on the work you do and questions from other members of your community asking how you managed to work with a certain person, or what you did to secure a certain feature. These are the people that you want to connect with, and it's your responsibility to help them grow their business.

Identify one or two competitors that you like and respect, but whose work differs from yours in a very specific, identifiable way. For example, if you specialize in ballroom weddings, seek out someone who loves working outdoors.

If you are known for boy band entertainment, find someone who leans more towards classic rock, or the 80's. It's important that they offer the same service, but that the art and the function is delivered differently.

Next, reach out and let them know that you want to talk about potentially referring business to them. This will come as a shock, as most professionals want to keep all of the business to themselves. Explain that there are times when you are unavailable, when you don't connect with a client, or when you simply cannot provide them with what they want, and tell your colleague (no longer a competitor) that you want to see if perhaps they would be a good fit.

Once you get a favorable response from someone who seems genuinely interested, set a meeting aimed at learning as much about their business as you can. Interview them in the same way a client would interview you, and note where the businesses diverge from one another. Ask questions about what the business operates the way it does, and ask what pain points the owner and manager currently has that you can help alleviate.

This is a vulnerable process and can put people in an uncomfortable position. No one likes to feel as if they are being judged, and in the beginning your counterpart may be reticent to share too much out of fear.

The best way to move past this is to be open and vulnerable yourself. Share a story about a problem that you had, and explain how you worked through it and found a successful way out. Suggest a book that may be helpful to your partner or, better yet, order it for them right then and there via Amazon. Offer to take a look at one of their proposals, or help them if they are shorthanded on an event.

Once you establish a level of trust, admit to your counterpart that there are times when you feel like a unicorn, all alone and by yourself. Tell them that you want to create a partnership and a connection so that you can work together to attract more of the right clients to your market. Tell them that there are times when you struggle, and it would mean a lot to have someone who understood your business that you could talk to, and that want to see them succeed. Success for one of us is success for all of us, and by strengthening the market as a whole you will attract more clients for each of you individually and for your local vendors.

Seek to come to an agreement with one another on certain terms. These are the Do's and Don'ts that will govern your relationship. For example, as simple as it sounds, DO NOT ever disparage, gossip about, or be dis-respectful with regards to the other person or their business. DO promise that anything you discuss during a phone call or lunch will not be repeated to anyone else. DO agree that you will refer clients who are not a good fit to your business to them first, if that client is legitimately a good fit for them. DO share learning and education that you each receive separately, and promise to always include the other in opportunities. DO NOT steal ideas from one another, and while you may share each other's work and success online as a way to support your market, DO NOT present it as if it were you own.

When I speak to business owners about the sharing of ideas

they immediately clam up, telling me that they do not want to reveal their secrets. Allow me to put this fear to rest once and for all. There are no industry secrets. There are just different people who see the world through totally different lenses, and who present their work in a very specific way.

Sharing my contract and explaining to another wedding planner how I structure my payment plans in no way helps them close business and "steal" a potential client. Instead, it sets an industry standard and provides our couples with a level of stability and trust. Two venues getting together to find a better way to present pricing does not hurt the other. Instead, it levels the playing field. D.J.s that come together and create a baseline of pricing do not undercut one another, but they raise the bar and set the standard of pricing for the industry. The practices are not injurious, and they certainly are not secret. Instead, by working together, competitors become colleagues who then set the industry standard, allowing potential couples to feel confident. Brides and grooms will always search out information from various sources, and in today's market the smart couple will educate themselves by speaking to a number of professionals. By creating your own competition and agreeing to behave in a certain way, you instill a level of confidence in your clients. Couples will come to understand that at a certain level the market operates in a very specific way.

If done right, creating your own competition will also make you better. By coming to terms and having a somewhat level playing field (whether that is on price, process, or delivery) you will be forced to compete solely on the merit of your work. You, therefore, must stand firmly by your artistic integrity. You must dig deep down into yourself and live in your place of why and how. Your marketing, your message, and your work will need to niche down into a very specific place where, despite the competition, you are the only choice that they can make. Clients are smart, and savvy, and those that try to pretend and fake it are exposed rather quickly these days. Therefore, instead of trying to mimic the style of your competition, create a partnership, work hard to grow together in professionalism and to foster education, and then take your style in as radically different a direction as possible.

In my own market, I have a colleague that I now consider a friend. We are both well educated in what we do, run sound businesses that approach many things in the same manner, we are both published and working with clients who work at a certain price point and that want a very specific experience. I go out of my way to answer any question she has, and I share everything with her fully and transparently. She has been a great source of support for me as well, and we meet up for lunch once every 6 weeks or so. Most of our lunches are about business, but we also sprinkle in a little family, friends, and industry at large talk. She and I do the same thing, and yet we are nothing alike. The style of our work is very different, and our personalities are very different, too. If you are attracted to the work she does and you like her designs, then you will not be attracted to mine.

The success we each have as individuals helps the other grow. When her work is published, a whole new set of eyes are attracted to Las Vegas. Some of them are only for her, but some of them find me. I share her work because I respect her, and also because I benefit from the success that she enjoys. If I have a question about a vendor she works with that I have not met, she is always willing to make the introduction. When one of my weddings catches the eye of her clients, and they ask for a special piece or element that I brought in from out of market, she calls me and I connect her with the right people. We cheer loudest for each other, always, and the work we do trickles down into our local market. These are the people I live near. Our husbands know one another. Our kids go to school together. Our city and our towns are made better by having a community of strong, successful, profitable businesses in operation.

Why would I not do everything to help the people in my own market succeed? Why "fear" competition when no one else can be me? Why not, instead, celebrate the differences in our businesses and our personalities, and use those to help both our clients and our colleagues move forward to create the best experiences for all.

There is power in community. You just have to see it.

GROWING PAINS

All businesses experience growing pains. For some of us, the pain is immediately acute. For others, it is barely noticeable at first. It may begin with you feeling slightly irritable, and you may get short and snappy with those closest to you. You might feel exhausted and want to sleep all the time. Or perhaps you cannot sleep, and you find yourself tossing and turning all night long. Generally speaking, there is just a sense of exhaustion and discontentment. You and your business are just off.

Suddenly, you are hit with the realization that something is truly wrong. This can come to you in a variety of ways. You make a mistake on a major account. You lose a piece of business that you absolutely should have closed. You look at your calendar and find you have a lot of holes that need to be filled.

Growth is painful, and never easy. I say this having been there.

In the year 2016, I produced nineteen weddings and events. In 2018, I produced two weddings. Just. Two.

What had I done to bring this on?

From the moment I started my business I was committed to taking as much business as I could. I very much felt that I, and the city of Las Vegas, had something to prove. As time went on I developed my personal style and standards for the work that I wanted to do, but the truth was I didn't always honor those standards.

As 2016 came to a close, I found that I was worn out, tired, stretched, and frustrated. Yes, I had done a lot of work that I just loved. Yes, my clients were all amazing individuals. Still, there was work that I was doing that I was not as invested in; clients I had taken on just to pay the bills. Other clients had a style that was so different from my own, I wondered why they had chosen me. I knew, of course, why I had taken them. Or I thought I did. I had a number of excuses masquerading as reasons. I needed to pay the bills. I wanted to prove that I was good. I had the date open, and if I did not fill the date it would just sit there, empty. Why not do the work and make some money? The result of taking less than ideal clients was work that was simply not as strong as it could have been.

The fault was mine. By trying to conform to every client, I failed to honor who I was. I was producing "Andrea Light" in an effort to meet my clients where they were, despite the fact that their goals that did not align with my own. I was acting like an admin, and not like an expert.

I had to stop. I decided that I could no longer afford to do anything that I didn't love. I had been taking on as much as I could to grow the business, and I loved my work so much. I truly wanted to do all of it, for everyone. But I am not for everyone, and with the help of peer-to-peer education, business coaching, and a good dose of courage I made the difficult decision to lean into the change, knowing that the business would take a hit.

How then did I find my way through the slow season in my business?

I can tell you what I did not do; I never bastardized the goals I had set. Nor do I recommend that you do. I did not down shift, I never changed my plan, and I did not start discounting services. I stayed the course, trusting that the business would provide, because the business always had.

At this point you are probably thinking, "That's great in an ideal world, but how do I pay the bills?"

Of all the challenges you will go through, this is the one that will rock you the hardest, because there are real world risks. The consequences of not having an influx of cash, especially if you have not prepared for this dip by putting away a sufficient amount of funds, can be dire. It puts your business in jeopardy, your rent, your family. Everything. But down-shifting, scaling back, and doing less than your best is what has put you in this difficult position to begin with.

The scary reality of this time is that there will be less

"business" in your business. These are the growing pains that cause many business to fold. By trying to do everything they can for every dollar, they ensure certain death. Which is why I want you to do something radically different.

Rather than attempt to stimulate volume through sales that force you to do half of your best, I want you to double down on the work you truly want to do. Go back to your original goals; revisit your why. You started this process in order to redefine your business. That is what you are doing. To walk away because things get hard disrespects and nullifies everything you have done up until now. Do not allow the hard times to stop you from reaching your goal.

You have done the hard work to redefine your business, and it has worked. The scope of your business is changing based on the steps you have taken, as outlined in this book.

Change, therefore, is inevitable, but growth is a choice. You can get through the process and come out stronger on the other side if you continue to commit to the process. You are almost there; I promise.

The first step in getting through this change is accepting where you are in the process. It has been said that, "The oldest and strongest emotion of mankind is fear, and the oldest and strongest kind of fear is fear of the unknown." (H. P. Lovecraft)

Too many business owners put on blinders and fail to acknowledge that things are changing because they are afraid to face the unknown. Do not be one of these people.

Instead, make a habit of checking in with yourself and your business every month. Schedule a calendar appointment if you have to, and review where your business stands in relation to your goals. Consider things such as how close are you to your revenue goals, the number of clients you have booked, and whether or not you are doing the type of work that you find most interesting.

Once you have a strong sense of where your business stands, you can face your challenges and your fears directly. Describe the gap and write out your challenges and your fears, but frame them as opportunities instead of issues.

Then, recommit to your education. Education is the key to success in our industry. The goal is to expose yourself to new ideas so that you can approach your business differently. Read everything you can get your hands on, enroll in an online course, or do an internship in another segment of the industry. Do not focus on being a better planner, designer, photographer, etc. Instead, focus on being a better business owner. Learn about accounting, publishing, employee management, or the law. Explore business strategies, read the classics, and listen to podcasts. The goal is to take in information from a wide variety of sources, and apply the information to your business in new and innovative ways.

Armed with new thought processes, focus on addressing the gaps by designing a pathway forward. You cannot afford to ignore that which is wrong with your business, and you cannot transform your business by doing what you have already done. Do not attempt to make yourself feel better by reducing the goal or aiming for an abbreviated version of what you really want. That is the easy way out. Instead, double down on who you are and what you believe. Take your vision for the future and magnify it. Go further, beyond niche, and push yourself to the border of obsessive. The more radical you are, the more committed you will become. Refuse to accept anything less than exactly what you want. Spread your message across all platforms, talk about it again and again on every platform you have.

Instead, brainstorm ways to address each issue that you are having. Focus on trial and error, knowing that most of what you do won't work. That's okay; you don't need it to. All you need is one tactic to take hold.

That tactic is diversification. Offer a new service based on the best of the best that you offer. Look at what you do best, and create an offering around that one, highly specialized and unique thing that you do better than anyone else. Perhaps you offer incredible customer service. If that is your specialty, create a program that allows you to teach other members of your community how to take care of their clients. Perhaps you are known for designing specularly over the top events. If this is your legacy, perhaps you can offer a modified service where you sell the design, but not the execution.

My downturn left a void where business used to be. Where once there was work, there was empty space and quiet. I learned, I read, and I put in real time with my partners. My slump was of my own doing, and I committed to working though it. I created new products for clients, new training programs for partners, and new marketing initiatives for myself. I took that which I believed in - my ability to redefine the wedding industry in Las Vegas - and I amplified by voice. I spoke louder, and longer, and in more places than I ever could. I dig my heels in, took corporate clients, created new products, and scaled back on every expense I had.

The final goal never changed, but the tactics I took in order to pivot did.

In many ways, the year 2018 was the hardest for me professionally. Emotionally, I was devastated. I wondered why I wasn't booking as quickly as my local colleagues. I was envious about the work that I was not getting. I looked at my vision board and my goals, and I wondered if I was ever going to get there. I asked myself (and my husband) how I had broken my business more times than I could count, and I questioned absolutely everything I ever knew.

At the same time, however, 2018 is also the year that I am the most proud of. For when I looked back, I realized that I wasn't envious of the work others were doing. It was work I didn't want to do. In fact, much of it was work that I had passed on a referred elsewhere because I didn't think it was a good fit. My largest goals were being met by the two perfect clients I had. They were allowing me the freedom to do the kind of work that I wanted to do while paying me the type of money that I wanted to make. The empty space that was left by clients that I truly did not want allowed me the latitude I needed to reevaluate my partnerships, developing stronger and deeper relationships with people who shared the same vision for the future that I had. I was given the opportunity to learn, to grow, and to create new things.

In times of stress and strife, revisit your goals. Reminded yourself of why you set yourself on this path.

The only way to truly be successful in business and in life is to live it on your own terms. That is what I did, and it is my greatest hope for you. When you approach your growing pains from this vantage point, you will realize that the situation you are in is not an issue, but an opportunity.

If you are not in this place yet, you will be. Growth and change are fraught with pain, drama, and uncertainty. There will be times when you will question everything that you are doing. Some things will work, many will not, and while you reach for a far away goal, there will be times when your business and your relationships suffer.

You will feel like giving up. You will want to quit. You will likely curse me and this book and this industry a thousand times before suddenly it all turns around. And that's OK. What is not okay is giving up.

Stay the course. You will come out on the other side.

DO IT AGAIN

If you are lucky, you can do it once.
If you are good, you can do it whenever you want.

Once your business is established it will take on a life of its own. The business itself becomes a living, breathing organism that will require constant care, attention, and management.

Never stop learning. Never stop growing. Always seek to redefine yourself and your market.

Because the world needs us.
And we need each other.

ACKNOWLEDGMENTS

My "overnight success" in this industry has been over twenty-five years in the making, but the true path to success started much earlier than that. I owe so much gratitude to those who have shaped and supported me along the way, and must take a moment to acknowledge the people who have made this possible.

To my mother and father. You believed I could, and so I did. Thank you for raising me to be relentless in the pursuit of all of my dreams. I love you, and everything I do is a reflection of the way in which I was raised.

To my sister and brother, Deanna and Tony. Put together by blood, we've stayed close through love. You have bore witness to my life from the beginning, and I am the luckiest to have had you by my side through it all.

To Pam Krohn. As a friend of your son, Mike Secker, I spent countless hours in your home. You took an interest in a 15 year old girl carrying around a binder filled with sketches and swatches for her Sweet 16. You confidently yet casually declared, "You should be a wedding planner," and in that moment set me on a path I didn't know existed. You unknowingly changed the course of my life and the lives of every person I have come in contact with since. For that you have my eternal gratitude.

To Rich Loska, my first professional mentor and life-long friend. Early in our relationship you said, "You've got balls, kid"; and you invested in teaching me how to use them. Leading by example, you taught me how to speak to people, how to say no, and how to be graceful under pressure. I learned that mentorship, management, and ownership is a lifetime process.

To Gary McCreary. You saw a 22 year old with hopes and dreams and you took me under your wing. You not only shared your office with me, but your knowledge. You set the bar high, pushing me to be better every day.

To Business Coach Sean Low, founder of The Business of Being Creative; you taught me how to think like a business and continue to encourage me in all of my outrageous endeavors. To our entire community at the BBC Collective, your influences will forever be felt in my business.

To every business and professional that has supported my vision over the years, your partnership has been invaluable to me. I am forever grateful to the teams at ARIA Las Vegas, The Bellagio Las Vegas, the Four Seasons Las Vegas, and the Mandarin Oriental Las Vegas which transformed itself beautifully into the Waldorf Astoria Las Vegas. Many thanks to my friends and creative partners at Butterfly Floral, By Dzign Destinations by Design, Javier Valentino Designs, Naakiti Floral, Palace Party Rentals, and RSVP Party Rentals for bringing my visions and sketches to life. None of which would be documents without the artistry of so many photographers and videographers, make up artists, entertainers, and partners; especially Adam Frazier Photography, AltF Photography, Brian Leahy Photography, DJ Brian Buonassissi, Dennis Kwan, Domenica Prestininzi, HOO Films, Jordan Kahn Orchestra, Le Reve Films, Lighten Films, Lovella Bridal Salon, Matthew Schenck and M Place Pro, Meldeen, DJ Nate Nelson Rene Zadori Photography, Stephen Salazar Photography, and Something New Films. If we have ever done any work together, then please know that you have in some way contributed to the creation of this book.

Beyond the work is education, support, and growth made possible only by the efforts of the following organizations. Rebecca Grinnals and Kathryn Arce are the founders of the Engage! Luxury Wedding Business Summit. This conference and community welcomed me into the rare air of professionals that are changing lives, one wedding at a time. You introduced me to the likes of Cindy Novotny and Simon T. Bailey, along with Brian Worley, Bob Conti, Ceci Johnson, Ed Libby, Jes Gordon, Mindy Weiss, Sharon Sacks and countless others whom have informed and inspired my work. To Susana Diharce, Bernadette Bailee, and the entire team at The Knot; thank you for championing me and my work.

To the members of the National Association for Catering and Events, the Wedding International Professionals Association (WIPA), the Wedding Planners Institute of Coordination (WPIC), The Wedding MBA, and CaterSource. The education you provide is invaluable to our industry. As someone who cares deeply about the growth of our industry I have always felt that I had something to say. Thank you for giving a platform from which to say it. To Brides, Carats & Cake, Glamour.com, Grace Ormonde Wedding Style Magazine, JuneBug.com, Inside Weddings, The New York Times, WedLuxe.com, and the many other publications that have shared my work over the years; I am forever in your debt.

To Alfonso Bernal, Ali Murray, Amanda Cohen Safarik, Amberly Collins, Andy Ebon, Angelica McDonnell, Arlene Barba, Brooke Palmer Kuhl, The Centereach Crew, Clara Hough, the late Clinton Clausen, Cherish and Lindsey Conklin, Corey Nyman, Couture Bride, Debby Jacobs Felker, Dan Gordon, Danielle Ghaffari Watson, Gurminder Banga, Jillian Peterson-Dukes, Jill Schneider, Jodi Harris, Joey D'Amore, Kaleigh Wiese, Kaitlin Collini, Kevin Cordova, Maria Nardi, Maris Roth, Marissa Kilkenny, Matthew Myhrum, Michelle Garibay, Mike Fox, Nayri Kalayjian, Nick Mitic, Nicole Peck, Paulina Clute, Reverend Peter Billitteri, Philip Van Nostrand, Rebecca Ickes, Rebecca Crumley, Rodney Arnett, Rocco Gonzalez, Tara Peeler, Tyra Bell Holland, Toby Cole, Tori Chivers, Vanessa Kelley, and Reverend William McFarland. Know what you mean to me, and that my journey means more for having you in it.

And lastly, to those that matter most…

Anthony and Alexandria. No words could ever tell you how much I love you. You have changed the world simply by being in it. Being your mama has been the greatest gift I have ever received, and I will fiercely defend you, love you, and champion everything about who you are for as long as I live. You are my heart, my way, and my why.

To "my Tony" - my partner in business and in life. In you, I have found everything that I ever wanted, but was too afraid to ask for. I am fascinated by how you see the world, and by how every motivation you have comes from being a good person and wanting to do the right thing. We have designed a life that is better than any story I could have hoped to write, and I will spend my days choosing you until the absolute end of time. I write this through tears, and words fail me. I can only say this…

I love you. Always.

ABOUT THE AUTHOR

Andrea Eppolito has dedicated her life to redefining what it means to celebrate life, luxury, and above all else…love, in the city of Las Vegas.

Born on Long Island, Andrea spent her teenage years moving between New York and Los Angeles. She relocated to Las Vegas in 1994, where she attended the University of Nevada Las Vegas where she earned a Bachelor of Science in Hospitality. After working with resorts, restaurants, and nightlife venues throughout the city, Andrea opened her wedding planning and event design business in 2011.

Andrea is renowned for bending the universe to her will (so to speak) and, in doing so, creating events that are both timely and timeless. She believes in lush, romantic details and offers an over the top interpretation of a client's world view. As such, Andrea is sought after by couples and corporation from around the globe who care deeply about production, transformation, and the art of story telling.

Andrea's first book, which showcases the beautiful weddings she has produced in Las Vegas, will be released in the fall of 2019. The book is a love letter to her city, and cements Las Vegas as a legitimate choice for couples planning opulent destination weddings.

Andrea is the founder of Wedding Editorialist. Based on the belief that every love story deserves to be told, Andrea and her team help couples and companies create custom magazines and advertorial marketing pieces.

Andrea travels the globe as a keynote speaker, encouraging businesses to tell better stories, operate with an intentional compass, and attract their ideal clientele. Her weekly podcast allows her discuss the struggles and successes of our industry, while her consulting and mentoring business focuses on developing sales and marketing strategies.

Called "vibrant, chic, and impeccably organized", Andrea is a voracious reader who devours business books, biographies, true crime, and romance novels. She loves doing anything with her husband, cooking at home for their kids, and traveling as a family.

ANDREA EPPOLITO
EDUCATION

A lifetime student and long time business coach, consultant, and educator, Andrea Eppolito Education is a division of Andrea Eppolito Events LLC that focuses on peer to peer education.

THE BUSINESS BLUEPRINT FOR
WEDDING PLANNERS

The Business Blueprint for Wedding Planners is a 4 HOUR CRASH COURSE that takes you step-by-step through the process of launching your own wedding planning business.

In this program, Andrea walks you through 10 Lessons, showing you exactly how to start your business.

This program is perfect for anyone who wants to start a business, or for a new business that wants to make sure they are set up absolutely perfectly!

BUSINESS BLUEPRINT
FOR
WEDDING PLANNERS

PRESENTING THE
WEDDING PLANNER
MASTERCLASS

THE WEDDING PLANNER MASTERCLASS

In The Wedding Planner Masterclass, Andrea takes you through the exact steps she used to expand her business, growing it from a small, local company to an internationally recognized brand that consistently attracts the right clients. In less than 5 Hours The Wedding Planner Masterclass will teach you how to do work that you are PASSIONATE about, that you can be PROUD OF, and that is PROFITABLE beyond your wildest dreams.

Don't settle for the business you have.
Go after the Business you WANT!

ONLINE RESOURCES

Subscribe to the Andrea Eppolito Events
YouTube Channel
www.youtube.com/c/AndreaEppolitoEvents

Listen to the Podcast!
Find Andrea Eppolito on iTunes, Spotify,
Stitcher, and more.

Do you want more education and information?
Visit us online for additional lessons,downloads,
and videos.
www.AndreaEppolito.com

LET'S CONNECT

Subscribe to the Andrea Eppolito NEWSLETTER:
www.AndreaEppolito.com

To BOOK Andrea Eppolito for Speaking or Consulting:
admin@andreaeppolito.com

READ the Andrea Eppolito Wedding Blog:
www.andreaeppolitoevents.com/blog

Tweet and FOLLOW along:
www.twitter.com/andreaeppolito

Do It For the 'GRAM:
www.instagram.com/andreaeppolito

Facebook FAN Page:
www.facebook.com/andreaeppolito